SpOil Your Pet

A Practical Guide to Using Essential Oils in Dogs and Cats

Mia K. Frezzo, DVM
Jan C. Jeremias, MSc.

©2014 by Jan Jeremias, MSc and Mia K. Frezzo, DVM

ISBN: 978-1-937702-23-6

Graphic Design: Samantha Kish

Printed and Bound in the U.S.A.

Dedications

I am forever grateful to Jan for changing my life by introducing me to essential oils. I dedicate this book to my children who inspired me to seek natural, safe and effective remedies for common ailments. Through those positive, empowering experiences, I began to expand my knowledge and use of essential oils for my veterinary patients. I feel proud to incorporate essential oils in my veterinary practice. I am entrusted with the health, well-being and happiness of my patients, and I feel confident achieving those goals using pure essential oils.

- Mia K. Frezzo, DVM

I am grateful to my parents and my friends and teachers for their support and love. I dedicate this book to my dog Kasey who showed me the power of essential oils and a complementary way of healing and wellness. This singular experience ignited a passion in me to incorporate essential oils in my life and to share my enthusiasm for this healing modality with others.

- Jan Jeremias, MSc

Mia K. Frezzo, DVM

Dr. Mia Frezzo is a veterinarian, wife and mother of three young children who resides in northern New Jersey. Her passion for veterinary medicine was initiated and fostered by her uncle, also a veterinarian, with whom she worked and studied since the age of 14. She graduated from The Ohio State University College of Veterinary Medicine in 1998 and returned home to New Jersey to practice veterinary medicine. She is the owner and medical director of the Animal Hospital of Hasbrouck Heights in Hasbrouck Heights, New Jersey. Dr. Frezzo's patients, primarily dogs and cats, benefit greatly from her combined holistic and traditional approach with an emphasis on natural health and prevention of illness.

Dr. Frezzo became convinced of the power of essential oils when the oils cured her 2 year old daughter of a chronic respiratory illness, and she no longer had to rely on a nebulizer and daily prescription medications. As Dr. Frezzo became increasingly frustrated with her daughter's lack of progress and dependence on medications, she sought other remedies. She turned to Jan for help. They had met at their local yoga studio, and she knew that Jan was knowledgeable in using essential oils and natural healthcare. Jan introduced Dr. Frezzo to the power of pure essential oils. Within just two weeks, her daughter's respiratory signs were fully resolved.

It was this profound experience that changed all of their lives greatly, including Dr. Frezzo's approach to the care of her patients. Since that encounter with essential oils, Dr. Frezzo has shared natural healthcare with her family, friends, clients and pets both in the United States and abroad. This experience also led to a greater friendship between Jan and Dr. Frezzo, and ultimately, to this book.

Jan C. Jeremias, MSc

Jan Jeremias, MSc. is a certified yoga teacher and reflexologist. She received a Bachelor's Degree in Biology from Stern College for Women and a Master's Degree in Immunology of Infectious Diseases and a Diploma in Tropical Medicine from the London School of Hygiene and Tropical Medicine- University of London. Jan worked in clinical infectious disease and cancer research centers at Cornell University Medical College and Mount Sinai Medical School in New York City for over 20 years and worked for the New York City Department of Health (NYCDOH) for 4 years.

While working for the NYCDOH, Jan was introduced to essential oils to help with her 14 year old dog, Kasey, who had Canine Cognitive Disorder or old dog "dementia". At first skeptical about the power and benefits of using essential oils, she soon became convinced when her dog began acting and feeling better and lived to the age of 19. Since then, Jan has completed extensive coursework in aromatherapy and essential oils for animals. Her passion for natural health and her scientific background has allowed her to help and heal people and their pets worldwide as she continues to share essential oils with family, friends, students, and clients.

Working and sharing essential oils with people has introduced Jan to many wonderful people, her two business partners and friends, Lillian Brenwasser and Denise Schwendeman and her co-author, dear friend and colleague, Mia Frezzo, without whom none of this would have been possible.

Acknowledgements

We would like to acknowledge Emily Wright, Connie and Alan Higley, Carrie and Fred Donegan, and Lillian Brenwasser for their support and guidance during the creation of this book.

TABLE OF CONTENTS

WELCOME

Welcome to SpOIL Your Pet: A Practical Guide to Using Essential Oils for Dog and Cat Owners.

We love our pets! They are family members, and they deserve only the best. We strive to give our pets the longest, healthiest lives possible and believe that the key to longevity is prevention of illness and maintenance of good health.

Dogs and cats race through life, entering adolescence at 4-7 months and beginning their golden years at age 7. To put it in perspective, they age an average of 6-10 years for each of our calendar years.

Always, follow your veterinarian's advice about protecting your pet from diseases, parasites and conditions prevalent in your area. We recommend a biannual physical examination for all dogs and cats. More frequent veterinary visits may be needed depending on the age of the pet and any particular medical condition(s) it may be facing.

We value annual blood work, even in healthy pets, to thoroughly evaluate and discover any illness or concern as early as possible. It is important to focus on maintaining good health and well-

I have felt cats rubbing their faces against mine and touching my cheek with claws carefully sheathed. These things, to me, are expressions of love.

- James Herriot

being as well as addressing any specific ailments. Blood tests and other diagnostic testing may be recommended more often for certain conditions. Greater success is achieved when instituted early in the course of a disease and when a combination of traditional and complementary veterinary medicine is used.

Prevention of disease or illness is imperative. In addition to regular veterinary visits and annual testing, provide high quality nutrition, supplements such as omega-3 fatty acids (fish oils) and a probiotic, and use essential oils to support your pet's immune system. Essential oils offer complementary therapy, enhancing other therapies and are best used under the supervision of a veterinarian. In some cases, essential oils may offer complete treatment or cure your pet's condition.

WHAT ARE ESSENTIAL OILS?

Both people and pets can benefit from the power of pure essential oils. Proven effective for hundreds of ailments, the history of essential oils dates back to ancient times when plants were the first medicines. Essential oils are not new, and modern society is returning to a safer, natural approach to illness and a rediscovery of essential oils.

Each essential oil contains specific benefits to which the body and mind respond. Essential oils are antiseptic and immune system stimulants. They fight viruses, bacteria, fungal organisms, tumors, and more. Essential oils are non-water based phytochemicals made up of volatile aromatic compounds. Although they are fat soluble, pure essential oils do not include fatty lipids or fatty acids, so they are immediately absorbed by the skin.

Essential oils are the volatile aromatic compounds found in the seeds, bark, stems, roots, flowers and other parts of plants. These potent oils, obtained from the steam distillation of plant material, give plants their characteristic aroma. In addition to giving plants their distinctive smells, essential oils are the plant's complex and unique defense system against predators and disease and play a role in its reproductive system.

Additionally, essential oils offer complementary therapy to traditional medicine. They do not have any side effects and usually do not interact with other medications your pet may be taking. We recommend only the use of certified pure therapeutic grade essential oils that are tested for purity and potency. Always consult your veterinarian when adding anything new to your pet's health care regimen.

HOW TO USE ESSENTIAL OILS

We only recommend and refer to 100% pure therapeutic grade essential oils in this book.

There are three ways to use 100% pure therapeutic grade essential oils.

They are:

1. Topically, by applying to the fur: Pure essential oils are potent, so 1-2 drops is a sufficient dose. Put 1-2 drops in your hand, gently rub your hands together, and pet your dog or cat. (Note: for cats, allow most of the oil to be absorbed into your hands. Then, pet your cat. Your cat has benefitted from the essential oil if you can smell it on him or her.) Petting your dog or cat anywhere on his or her body will be effective as essential oils are readily absorbed into the skin (See Guidelines for Using Essential Oils for dilution instructions). It is more effective to use smaller, more frequent doses of oils than to apply too many drops at one time. We recommend that you don't exceed 4 drops at one time. Some pets may appreciate the oils being applied to the abdomen or paws. For most, apply the oils to the back of the neck or back.

2. Aromatically using a diffuser: A diffuser breaks the essential oil into very small particles, which enter the air and are inhaled. There are two types of diffusers that we recommend. One is a water diffuser that disperses the essential oil into the air with moisture. By using a water diffuser, you can measure the number of drops and observe your pet's response. If your pet seems comfortable, you may opt to add more drops for the next session. A water diffuser allows you to combine several single oils easily.

The other type is a nebulizer diffuser, which requires little maintenance or cleaning. The amount of essential oil dispersed into the air is controlled easily with a dial. Start with the intensity setting on low and observe your pet's response.

Pure essential oils should not be heated or burned. These techniques destroy the therapeutic properties of the oil.

When diffusing for the first time, diffuse for 10 minutes and monitor your pet. If your pet shows signs of discomfort such as lethargy, increased breathing rate, panting, salivating, squinting eyes, or any other change that you consider to be adverse or out of the ordinary, simply turn off the diffuser and air out the space by opening windows and doors to let in plain fresh air.

3. Orally: High quality pure essential oils may be ingested Essential oils may be placed in capsules or in food, but we recommend adding essential oils to a dog's drinking water for ease of administration. Topical and aromatic uses are just as effective, or more so in certain cases, than oral administration. We do not recommend giving cats essential oils orally.

"HOT" OILS

A few oils produce a warming sensation in the body that may cause sensitivity. Hot oils include Cassia, Cinnamon, Clove, Melaleuca, Oregano, and Thyme. These oils should be diluted prior to application for dogs. With repeated use, as your dog becomes accustomed to the oil, the amount of dilution may be decreased gradually. Hot oils should only be used in cats under extreme circumstances and under the supervision of a veterinarian.

NO-NO'S

NEVER put essential oils directly in the eyes or ears of your dog or cat. In the event that an essential oil enters the eyes, immediately apply fractionated coconut oil or organic olive oil directly to the eyes. Do NOT rinse or flush the eyes with water as this will not remove the essential oil.

ESSENTIAL OILS IN CATS

Cats are very sensitive to oils and the quality of the essential oil is vital to its safe use. Pure, therapeutic grade essential oils are well tolerated by cats. There are some essential oils that are controversial, such as Melaleuca and Wintergreen, which are available from a wide variety of sources, and the quality of some of these oils may be questionable thereby affecting their safe use. In this book, we refer only to 100% pure therapeutic grade essential oils.

In general, when using oils on cats, we recommend beginning with milder oils, and only turning to stronger oils if necessary. When using "hot" oils in cats, we recommend diluting hot oils heavily or delivering their benefits via diffusing or by adding them to the litter box (See Litter Box Power, See Dilution Guide below). We recommend that you work in conjunction with your veterinarian when using "hot" oils, even if they are diluted.

GUIDELINES FOR USING ESSENTIAL OILS

• Always use 100% pure therapeutic or medicinal grade essential oils.

• Dilute essential oils in organic oils or lotions. Do not dilute essential oils in chemically laden lotions, soaps or shampoos. We recommend diluting with the carrier oil called fractionated coconut oil (FCO). FCO is an odorless, thin oil that is absorbed into the skin readily. FCO allows distribution of an essential oil over a greater portion of the body, if desired. For example, when treating pain.

• Dilution Guide for dogs: For puppies less than 8 weeks of age, dilute 1-2 drops of essential oil in 1 ounce (2 Tablespoons) of carrier oil. For small or toy breeds (weighing less than 20 pounds), dilute 2 drops in 1 ounce (2 Tablespoons) of carrier oil. For medium to large dogs (weighing more than 20 pounds), most essential oils can be applied undiluted. For elderly dogs (greater than 12 years of age), consider diluting essential oils using 2 drops in 1 ounce (2 Tablespoons) of carrier oil. Always dilute hot oils 1 drop of essential oil in 1-2 ounces (2-4 Tablespoons) of carrier oil.

• Dilution Guide for cats: For kittens (weighing less than 6 pounds and for elderly cats older than 10), dilute 1 drop of essential oil in (4 Tablespoons) of carrier oil. Always dilute hot oils 1 drop of essential oil in 2 ounces (4 Tablespoons) of carrier oil. To apply essential oils to your kitten or cat put 1-2 drops of undiluted oil or diluted oil in your hand, gently rub your hands together allowing most of the oil to be absorbed, and pet your cat's body. Your cat has benefitted from the essential oil if you can smell it on him or her.

• Pure essential oils do not stain clothing or bedding. A carrier oil may stain fabrics and may cause damage to finished wood surfaces. Additionally, carrier oils may make your pet's hair coat sticky or knotted and may be transferred to the rugs or furniture. Very few oils in this book are recommended to be used in a diluted fashion.

• Remember, essential oils are very concentrated. It is best to apply small amounts more frequently than a lot of oil all at once.

• Epileptic and seizure-prone dogs and cats are of special concern. It is believed that certain oils-Rosemary, Fennel, Sage, Eucalyptus, Hyssop, and Camphor are not recommended for use in animals with this condition. The reason is that these essential oils may trigger seizures in some people with epilepsy. While it has not been clinically researched, it has been observed in a variety of cases. Therefore, these oils should be used with caution in pets with epilepsy or a history of seizures. We suggest substituting Frankincense for Eucalyptus when treating pets with respiratory issues who also have a seizure disorder. Support digestive issues in pets with a seizure disorder by using Lavender and Myrrh.

• Care must be taken with pets who have bleeding disorders, difficulty clotting or who are taking anticoagulant therapy. If your pet is taking medication for a bleeding disorder and you wish to add essential oils to their health regimen, we suggest you include your veterinarian in this decision. In these pets, avoid topical application of Wintergreen, Cassia, Blue Tansy, Fennel, Clove, Cinnamon, Oregano, and Sweet Birch. Diffusing the above oils is safe (example, Protective Blend, which contains clove and cinnamon). When treating pain in pets with bleeding disorders, we suggest substituting Massage Blend, Helichrysum, Geranium or Lavender for Soothing Blend which contains Blue Tansy and Wintergreen. When treating an infection for a pet with a bleeding disorder, choose Myrrh, Helichrysum, Frankincense or Lavender instead of Oregano. Support digestive issues in pets with bleeding disorders using Lavender and Myrrh rather than Digestive Blend.

• A pregnant dog and cat are special, and therefore care should be taken when using oils during pregnancy. The guidelines for using essential oils during human pregnancy, we feel are also relevant for pregnancy in pets. Oils that would be better used diluted with a carrier oil during pregnancy: Clove, Cypress, Eucalyptus, Ginger, Marjoram, Oregano, Peppermint. The following oils should only be used in consultation with your veterinarian: Basil, Cassia, Cinnamon Bark, Clary Sage, Lemongrass, Rosemary, Thyme, Vetiver, Wintergreen, White Fir. Use peppermint essential oil sparingly near the end of pregnancy and while breastfeeding. Mint is known to decrease milk production.

"I hope to make people realize how totally helpless animals are, how dependent on us, trusting as a child must that we will be kind and take care of their needs."

- James Herriot

HOW TO USE THIS BOOK

This book is organized to provide dog and cat owners with information about essential oils and how to use them on their dogs and cats. The information is easy to access and gives pet owners practical tools to keep their dogs and cats healthy and to address common medical conditions and ailments using essential oils.

Most essential oils can be used effectively for multiple conditions. In other words, no one oil has just one purpose. In this book, the essential oil(s) we suggest for a particular condition, are our favorites based on scientific research and personal knowledge and experience.

The chapters are as follows: Introduction, Conditions and Ailments, Common Essential Oils, Recipes, and References.

Each section, contains a brief description of a medical ailment or condition, listed in alphabetic order, our recommendations for that condition, and clear instructions for how to use the oils. At the end of each ailment or condition segment is the "What Do I Do section?". Here, are precise guidelines on what to do in this situation for dogs and/or cats. At the end of each ailment or condition are precise guidelines on what to do in this situation for dogs and/or cats.

Color Coding:

The Dog section color

The Cat section color

If the recommendations apply to both Dogs and Cats

Symbols:

Look for these unique icons to indicate information for Dogs, Cats, both Dogs and Cats, Emergency, and Caution. The icons will help you to quickly and easily locate methods of essential oil use, such as topical application, diffusing, or oral use for a particular situation for your dog or cat.

FOR DOGS

FOR CATS

FOR DOGS & CATS

FOR EMERGENCY
AND CAUTION

Part of being a pet owner is learning about your individual pet. This book will empower you to help them stay healthy and to take care of their health needs as they arise.

We hope you enjoy this book!

ABSCESSES

An abscess is a pus-filled infected pocket typically located beneath the skin. Most commonly, cats develop abscesses from wounds incurred by other cats. Outdoor cats firmly defend their territory, and males fight over females. A bite or a scratch from a cat deposits tremendous amounts of bacteria beneath the surface of the skin. Dogs more often suffer wounds from fences, playing with other dogs or fighting.

An abscess is generally a raised, warm, painful area of the body. Pets with abscesses are often ill and may develop a fever. They may become lethargic and lose their appetite. If you notice a swelling or painful area of the skin, or your pet is sick, contact your veterinarian immediately.

At home, when you first suspect an abscess, clean the area with a natural cleanser (See Gentle Cleanser). Apply warm compresses using a wash cloth soaked in very warm water containing 2-3 drops of Lavender oil for 3-5 minutes 2-4 times daily. Pat the area dry, and apply Healing Salve (See recipe) 2-4 times daily. The abscess will come to a head, open and drain pus and blood. Once the abscess opens and drains, the pet may feel better, but still see your veterinarian. If the abscess does not open the veterinarian may need to lance, drain, or flush the abscess and treat your pet with antibiotics and pain relief.

Essential oils can complement traditional therapies and support the immune system to aid healing. Continue to keep the affected area clean and medicated with ointment (See Healing Salve).

For dogs, apply Oregano (diluted) twice daily. Apply Melaleuca near the wound twice daily. Diffuse Protective Blend. Feed your pet a healthy diet supplemented with Omega-3 and probiotics.

For cats, apply Lavender, Melaleuca (diluted) and Myrrh twice daily. Diffuse Protective Blend. Feed your pet a healthy diet supplemented with Omega-3 and probiotics.

FOR DOGS

Apply 1 drop Oregano (diluted 1 drop in 2 Tbsp. carrier oil) twice daily.

Apply 1 drop Melaleuca (diluted 1 drop in 2 Tbsp. carrier oil), near the wound twice daily.

Coat the affected area with Healing Salve twice daily.

Diffuse Protective Blend for 20-30 minutes 2-3 times daily.

Feed your dog a healthy diet supplemented with Omega-3 and probiotics.

FOR CATS

Apply 1 drop Melaleuca (diluted 1 drop in 4 Tbsp. carrier oil), near the wound twice daily.

Apply 1 drop each Lavender and Myrrh twice daily for cats.

Coat the affected area with healing Salve twice daily.

Diffuse Protective Blend for 20-30 minutes 2-3 times daily.

Feed your cat a healthy diet supplemented with Omega-3 and probiotics.

FOR DOGS & CATS

Clean the affected area 1-2 times daily with Gentle Cleanser.

Apply warm compresses using a wash cloth soaked in very warm water containing 2-3 drops of Lavender oil for 3-5 minutes 2-4 times daily. Pat the area dry.

Lavender & Chamomile

Gentle Skin Cleanser

4 ounces Castile soap or unscented natural foaming soap

2 drops Roman Chamomile Essential Oil

2 drops Lavender Essential Oil

Myrrh

Healing Salve

8 ounces Cold-Pressed Organic Coconut Oil

1 ounce Beeswax

2 drops Vitamin E (optional)

10 drops Lavender Essential Oil

5 drops Myrrh Essential Oil

3 drops Helichrysum Essential Oil

Glass Jars or Tin Containers

Place the coconut oil and beeswax over a double –boiler, and gently warm over low heat until the beeswax melts. Remove from heat and add the essential oils and Vitamin E oil, (if using). Quickly pour the mixture into glass jars or tins, and allow to cool completely. Store salve in a cool location where it will not re-melt and re-solidify. When stored correctly, salve will last for 1-3 years. Yields 8 oz.

ACID REFLUX

Does your pet vomit yellow fluid and foam in the mornings or when he or she has not eaten for an extended period of time? This behavior may indicate acid reflux. See your veterinarian for an examination and routine diagnostic testing, such as bloodwork and x-rays.

Once the diagnosis of acid reflux is confirmed, apply Digestive Blend and give your pet a probiotic supplement to provide, healthy digestive bacterial flora, facilitate digestion and support a strong immune system (See Nutrition).

FOR DOGS

Apply 1-2 drops of Digestive Blend twice daily.

Give your dog a probiotic supplement daily.

FOR CATS

Apply 1 drop of Digestive Blend daily.

Give your cat a probiotic supplement daily.

Ginger, found in a digestive blend.

A dog is the only thing on earth that loves you more than you love yourself.

- Josh Billings

ADDISON'S DISEASE

(Hypoadrenocorticism/Adrenal Insufficiency)

Addison's disease is an endocrine disorder characterized by decreased production of adrenal hormones, particularly cortisol. Both dogs and cats can develop Addison's disease, yet it is more common in dogs and extremely rare in cats. Pets with Addison's disease show severe weakness, anorexia, excessive thirst, vomiting and diarrhea. Addison's disease can be very serious and life-threatening. It is most often caused by an immune-mediated disorder.

Spruce, found in a grounding blend

If you notice any of the above signs, contact your veterinarian. Addison's disease is usually diagnosed by your veterinarian using blood and urine tests and ultrasonography.

When a pet is stressed, their adrenal glands produce cortisol, which helps them deal with the stress. Pets that have Addison's disease cannot make enough cortisol. Therefore, in stressful situations, their symptoms may worsen. Sources of stress vary based on the breed, temperament and personality. Any change in the day-today routine, house guests, new baby or new pet is stressful and may worsen the signs of Addison's disease or lead to an Addisonian crisis in which signs of weakness, vomiting and diarrhea are very severe. An Addisonian crisis is an emergency. Call your veterinarian.

Support traditional therapy with essential oils. To help with lack of appetite, vomiting and diarrhea, apply Digestive Blend to the abdomen and diffuse Invigorating Blend. To assist in cleansing the liver, kidneys, and bladder, apply Detoxification Blend. To support the immune system and maintain overall health, diffuse Protective Blend. Apply Frankincense and Grounding Blend twice daily to help balance the emotions and the energy of the body. Apply Invigorating Blend or Calming Blend for tranquility. Continue to support overall health by feeding a high quality diet and supplementing Omega-3 and probiotics.

FOR DOGS

Apply 1-2 drops Digestive Blend to the abdomen twice daily.

Apply 1 drop Detoxification Blend daily.

Apply 1 drop each Frankincense and Grounding Blend twice daily.

Diffuse Invigorating Blend or Calming Blend for 20-30 minutes 2-3 times daily.

Diffuse Protective Blend for at least 20-30 minutes 2-3 times daily.

Continue to support overall health by feeding a high quality diet and supplementing Omega-3 and probiotics.

Note: A pet with Addison's disease is delicate and can worsen acutely at any time, especially in response to stress. Contact your veterinarian immediately if you notice lethargy, vomiting, diarrhea or increased thirst in your pet.

ALLERGIES

Allergens and irritants are present everywhere in our environment. Pets may be sensitive to grasses, trees, shrubs, pollen, foods, medications, insect bites, fragrances and cleaning products. Allergic pets commonly have red, itchy skin especially affecting the face, ears, paws and rectum. Itchy pets will scratch, rub, roll, lick and bite themselves, scoot, and shake their heads.

Addressing seasonal, environmental, or food allergies will help many of the secondary conditions such as ear or skin infections to heal. (See Skin Infections, Ear Infections, Spider Bites, Nutrition)

Peppermint

Allergic pets may scratch so much that they cause skin lesions and open wounds. Skin infections may be treated with an antibacterial/antifungal shampoo (See Soothing Skin Shampoo) followed by applying Lavender and Melaleuca (dilute in cats).

Lavender is a natural antihistamine, anti-inflammatory and an anti-infectious agent. Lavender also helps to repair the skin. Melaleuca (diluted in cats) has been documented to kill many bacteria, viruses, and fungi on contact so it is excellent as an antiseptic for pets with itchy skin. Diffusing Protective Blend, Cleansing Blend, or Frankincense is helpful in killing environmental molds and in preventing infection in your home.

FOR DOGS

Apply 1-2 drops Lavender 2-3 times daily.

(In an acute case of an allergic reaction, such as an insect bite, 1-2 drops Lavender may be safely applied hourly, if needed.) (See Spider Bites, Fleas, Ticks and Mosquitoes)

Apply 1-2 drops Melaleuca twice daily for secondary skin infections (See Cuts and Scrapes).

Combine one drop each of Lavender, Lemon and Peppermint in an empty vegetable capsule and administer by mouth 2-4 times daily. Alternatively, combine 1 drop each Lavender, Lemon and Peppermint and apply 2-4 times daily.

Diffuse Cleansing Blend, Frankincense or Protective Blend for 20-30 minutes 2-3 times daily.

Bathe with natural Soothing Skin Shampoo (See recipe).

FOR CATS

Apply 1 drop each Lavender and Myrrh daily.

Diffuse Cleansing Blend, Frankincense or Protective Blend for 20-30 minutes 2-3 times daily.

Bathing cats can be challenging. We suggest you find a groomer that specializes in cats and have your groomer use the natural Soothing Skin Shampoo (See recipe).

Lavender

Soothing Skin Shampoo

3 oz. Castile soap (available at many health and bulk food stores)

2 oz. Organic unpasteurized, unfiltered Apple Cider Vinegar

1 oz. Vegetable Glycerin

2 oz. Distilled water

3 drops Lavender Essential Oil

3 drops Roman Chamomile Essential Oil

Optional: add 1 tsp. ground oatmeal

ANAL GLANDS

The anal glands are located on either side of the rectum at the 4 o'clock and 8 o'clock positions. They should be emptied naturally with each bowel movement and serve as an identification source for other dogs and cats. In cases of diarrhea, constipation, seasonal allergies or food allergies, these glands may become full, painful, infected or abscessed. It is important to identify the root cause, if possible, and address it promptly (See Diarrhea and Vomiting, Nutrition, Allergies).

> *What we have once enjoyed we can never lose. All that we love deeply becomes a part of us."*
>
> *- Helen Keller*

To reduce the pain and inflammation associated with the anal glands, apply homemade Healing Spray and Healing Oil Blend (See recipes). In some cases, the anal glands may need to be expressed by your veterinarian. If your pet is prone to anal gland issues, continue using the natural spray or oil blend. If you can see a red, painful bulge at the side of the rectum or the tissue has ruptured, contact your veterinarian.

FOR DOGS & CATS

Spray a mixture of Healing Spray and follow with an application of Healing Oil Blend up to 3-4 times daily.

Helichrysum

Healing Spray and Healing Oil Blend

4 ounce glass spray bottle

15 drops Frankincense Essential Oil

10 drops Oregano Essential Oil (substitute Geranium Essential Oil for cats)

10 drops Lavender Essential Oil

10 drops Helichrysum Essential Oil

4 ounces of water for the spray

OR

100 drops of carrier oil such as Fractionated Coconut Oil

For dogs only: If no relief is noted in 24 hours, add 5 drops of Protective Blend to the Healing Spray and Healing Oil Blend.

For any condition that persists or worsens, contact your veterinarian.

ANOREXIA AND LOSS OF APPETITE

A pet may refuse to eat or eat less than normal for any number of reasons. In general, one or two days of decreased appetite is not alarming. It is not uncommon and usually insignificant for a pet to turn its nose up at food for a brief period of time, but if this occurs for more than 3 days, it is time to pay attention to the problem and contact your veterinarian.

Many times, there may be a simple explanation such as stress (See Anxiety and Stress). In other cases, eating garbage or having a taste of table food can lessen a pet's interest in their own food. However, a number of more serious medical conditions can interfere with a pet's appetite. If loss of appetite or complete refusal to eat persists for three or more days, contact your veterinarian.

Important: If you suspect that your pet has swallowed a foreign object, string, toy, clothing, coin, chemical or toxin, contact your veterinarian immediately. Pets with a foreign body in them usually do not eat.

Anise, found in a digestive blend

For simple cases of indigestion or overeating, apply Digestive Blend or Lavender and Myrrh essential oils. Diffuse citrus essential oils because citrus oils stimulate the digestive system and are uplifting. Probiotic supplements are very helpful for digestive conditions. If your pet already takes a probiotic, consider increasing the dose for a day or two.

FOR DOGS

Apply 1-2 drops of Digestive Blend or 1 drop each Lavender and Myrrh oils 2-4 times daily, as needed.

Diffuse a citrus essential oil in the area where your dog eats.

Give your dog a probiotic supplement daily.

FOR CATS

Apply 1 drop Digestive Blend or 1 drop each Lavender and Myrrh oils 1-2 times daily, as needed.

Add Digestive Blend to the litter box as described in Litter Box Power.

Diffuse a citrus essential oil in the area where your cat eats.

Give your cat a probiotic supplement daily.

ANXIETY AND STRESS

Pets become anxious for a number of reasons. Has your pet ever run under the bed during a thunderstorm, trembled as holiday guests arrive or relentlessly licked at his paw or leg? Does your cat vocalize the entire drive to the veterinary office? These situations are frightening to our pets. Often pets respond by causing damage to the home or themselves, hiding, becoming destructive or having bathroom accidents indoors or outside of the litter box for cats. Additional signs of anxiety in pets include vocalization, pacing, restlessness, panting, and salivation.

Another source of anxiety is traveling. Many pets travel to visit family or friends or to stay at boarding kennels while the family vacations or during holidays. Many dogs and cats feel anxious about spending even a short time in the car. Other pets may travel via an airplane.

Calm and soothe your pet with essential oils starting a few days prior to the event. Applying or diffusing lavender has been shown to inexpensively, safely and effectively reduce pet anxiety. Diffuse Lavender or Calming Blend, Grounding Blend or Frankincense in the home for 30-60 minutes prior to departure. For long drives, a car diffuser is quite handy. Depending on the length of travel and degree of anxiety, some pets may need reapplication of essential oil periodically.

Does your pet have a favorite blanket, bed or toy? Place a few drops of Calming Blend, Lavender or Grounding Blend on the object to comfort your pet. Drip essential oils on the towel or blanket in your cat's carrier. Apply on yourself the same essential oil you are using to calm your pet and act as a human diffuser. The pet will associate the aroma with you and will feel calmer and more secure.

Add a calming essential oil to the cat's litter box(es) as described in Litter Box Power. If you are boarding your pet with a boarding facility, family member or friend, ask if you may bring a diffuser to calm your pet while you are away.

Marjoram, found in a calming blend

FOR DOGS & CATS

Apply 1 drop Calming Blend, or 1 drop each Lavender and Grounding Blend or 1 drop Frankincense as often as hourly to ease signs of anxiety.

Diffuse Calming Blend, Lavender, Grounding Blend, or Frankincense for 30-60 minutes prior to a stressful event, before departure and in the car.

Apply 1-2 drops Calming Blend, Lavender and/or Grounding Blend on your pet's blanket, towel or toys.

Add a calming essential oil to the litter box as described in Litter Box Power.

ARTHRITIS

Many pets slow down as they age and exhibit signs of arthritis. Arthritis develops with age, conformational abnormalities such as hip dysplasia, patellar luxations and as a result of joint injuries or surgeries.

If your pet is overweight, start with a weight loss program including a proper diet, nutrition and exercise (See Nutrition). Essential Fatty Acids, also known as fish oil, specifically prepared for pets, reduces inflammation and supports the immune system. Additionally, pet supplements containing chondroitin sulfate, glucosamine and MSM are quite helpful. Supplements and natural alternatives can replace or lessen the necessity for traditional medications in many cases.

Essential oils have been found to reduce pain, inflammation and stiffness. Topical application of either Soothing Blend or Lavender and Frankincense essential oils may help to relieve discomfort in your pet. Soothing Blend is a combination of Wintergreen, Camphor, Peppermint, Blue Tansy, German Chamomile, Helichrysum, and Osmanthus, and not only relieves pain but also helps to repair injured tissue.

FOR DOGS

Apply 1-2 drops of Soothing Blend or equal parts of Lavender and Frankincense to the palms of your hands, and simply pet your dog. Pet the area of concern or anywhere on your pet's body 2-4 times daily as needed.

FOR CATS

Dilute 1 drop of Soothing Blend in 4 Tbsp. of carrier oil and apply 1-2 drops 2-4 times daily or apply 1 drop each of Lavender and Frankincense 2-4 times daily. Simply apply the oils to the palms of your hands, and pet your cat. Pure essential oils are absorbed into the bloodstream readily, so your pet will benefit even if you do not apply directly to the area of concern.

AUTOIMMUNE DISORDERS

Autoimmune disorders are difficult to understand. Suddenly and many times for no apparent reason, the body begins to attack itself. What? It sounds crazy, but it is true. Sometimes the organ of attack is a blood cell type, such as the red blood cells. In other cases, autoimmune disorders may cause skin lesions. Because of the variety of signs, bring your pet to your veterinarian whenever you notice unusual changes in their appearance or behavior. Some signs are bruises or areas of hemorrhage in the skin and gums, non-healing skin wounds, and lethargy. Any of these conditions require diagnostic testing, treatment and monitoring by your veterinarian. In addition, essential oils offer your pet complementary therapy by controlling infection and strengthening the immune system. Support your pet's immune system and healing with a healthy diet, and omega 3 and probiotic supplements.

For dogs, apply Frankincense, Grounding Blend and Helichrysum daily and diffuse Protective Blend or Lemon. These oils help to heal skin conditions, support the immune system and relieve tension and anxiety.

For Cats, apply Helichrysum, Frankincense, and Myrrh and diffuse Protective Blend or Lemon. These oils help to heal skin conditions, support the immune system and relieve tension and anxiety.

FOR DOGS

Apply 1-2 drops each of Frankincense,
Grounding Blend and Helichrysum twice daily.

Diffuse Protective Blend or Lemon.

Feed a healthy diet and supplement with omega-3 and
probiotics.

FOR CATS

Apply 1 drop each Frankincense, Helichrysum and Myrrh 1-2
times daily.

Diffuse Protective Blend or Lemon.

Feed a healthy diet and supplement with omega-3 and
probiotics.

BARTONELLA (CAT SCRATCH FEVER)

Bartonella is a bacterial disease contagious to people and very common among cats. In fact, about 30% of healthy cats are carriers of this disease yet show no signs of illness. Bartonella is spread by fleas and ticks (See Fleas, Ticks and Mosquitoes). Dogs rarely become infected with Bartonella.

Bartonella can affect many body systems, so the signs may be varied and include conjunctivitis, sneezing, runny nose, gingivitis, oral ulcers, heart disease, diarrhea, vomiting, fever and dermatitis.

Because Bartonella is so widespread among healthy cats, blood testing is recommended on all cats with or without signs of illness. We suggest testing when a new cat or kitten is acquired to ensure that your pet and family are protected from this contagious disease. Keeping your cat indoors and free of fleas and ticks (See Fleas, Ticks, and Mosquitoes) will help to protect your cat from contracting Bartonella.

Bartonella is treated with antibiotics, if the test result is positive. Essential oils provide complimentary therapy by helping to support your pet's immune system and assist in their recovery from Bartonella and any secondary illnesses that may develop. Essential oils will also help to protect you, your family and anyone who may come into contact with your infected pet while antibiotic therapy is completed.

For rare cases of Bartonella in dogs, apply Oregano Oil (diluted) daily. Apply Myrrh and Lavender oil twice daily. For respiratory symptoms, apply or diffuse Respiratory Blend. To support the immune system, diffuse Protective Blend. For cats, apply Frankincense daily. Apply Myrrh and Lavender oil twice daily.

For respiratory symptoms, apply or diffuse Respiratory Blend. To support the immune system, diffuse Protective Blend.

FOR DOGS

We suggest testing when acquiring a new dog to ensure that your pet and family are protected from this contagious disease.

Dilute 2 drops of Oregano in 2 Tablespoons of carrier oil. Apply 1 drop of diluted Oregano 2 times daily.

Apply 1 drop each Myrrh and Lavender once to twice daily.

Apply 1 drop Respiratory Blend twice daily.

Alternate diffusing Protective Blend or Respiratory Blend for 20-30 minutes 2-3 times daily.

FOR CATS

We suggest testing when acquiring a new cat to ensure that your pet and family are protected from this contagious disease.

Apply 1 drop Frankincense twice daily.

Apply 1 drop each Myrrh and Lavender twice daily

Apply 1 drop Respiratory Blend twice daily.

Alternate diffusing Protective Blend or Respiratory Blend for 20-30 minutes 2-3 times daily.

BROKEN BONES/BONE PAIN

In the event of a broken bone, see your veterinarian immediately. Essential oils can be used to speed healing and reduce inflammation once the fracture is repaired or set.

Apply, Soothing blend. It is a combination of Wintergreen, Camphor, Peppermint, Blue Tansy, German Chamomile, Helichrysum, and Osmanthus, and not only relieves pain but also helps to repair injured tissue. Apply, Grounding Blend, Lavender and Calming Blend to help ease anxiety and keep you and your pet calm.

Healing requires a strong immune system, proper hydration, and good nutrition. Support your pet by providing essential oils, high quality nutrition, a probiotic, and omega supplements.

FOR DOGS

Apply 1-2 drops of Soothing Blend and 1-2 drops of Helichrysum near the fracture area 2-3 times daily. After 1-3 weeks, decrease the frequency to 1-2 times daily.

Apply 1-2 drops of Grounding Blend twice daily.

Diffuse Lavender or Calming Blend 20-30 minutes for 2-3 hours.

FOR CATS

Dilute 1 drop of Soothing Blend in 4 Tbsp of carrier oil. Apply 1-2 drops of diluted Soothing Blend and 1-2 drops of Helichrysum near the fracture area 2-3 times daily. After 1-3 weeks, decrease the frequency to 1-2 times daily.

Apply 1-2 drops of Grounding Blend twice daily.

Diffuse Lavender or Calming Blend 20-30 minutes for 2-3 hours.

BURNS

Pets suffer from two main types of burns: thermal and chemical burns. Thermal burns are heat-related such as touching the stove, lying on the radiator, or overexposure to a heating pad. Chemical burns are from caustic substances such as irritants, acids or bases. Some common causes of chemical burns include car battery acid, cleaning products, bleach, ammonia, denture cleaner, teeth whitening products and pool chlorinating products. Chemicals cause harm through contact, inhalation (breathing in fumes) or ingestion.

In the event of a burn, remove the pet from the source of heat or chemical. Rinse the skin or affected part of his or her body for 10-20 minutes under COOL running water. Cover the affected area with a clean, soft, dry cloth and **SEEK VETERINARY CARE IMMEDIATELY.** Do NOT apply butter, ointments or Vaseline to burns. Do NOT apply ice to burns. If you have assistance, apply Lavender or Calming Blend to you and your pet to help keep you both calm.

After your pet has seen your veterinarian, apply Lavender, Frankincense and Healing Salve daily. Add Lemon to drinking water (if there are no cats in the home).

Alternate diffusing Protective Blend, Lavender, or Calming Blend daily.

SEEK VETERINARY ATTENTION IMMEDIATELY.

FOR DOGS & CATS

Apply 1-2 drops of Lavender or Calming Blend (Only if Time Permits).

After your pet has seen your veterinarian:
Apply 1-2 drops each Lavender and Frankincense 2-4 times daily.

Apply Healing Salve 2-4 times daily. (See recipe)

Add Lemon to drinking water (if there are no cats in the home).

Diffuse Protective Blend for 20-30 minutes at least 2-3 times daily.

Diffuse Lavender or Calming Blend for 20-30 minutes at least 2-3 times daily.

Lavender

Healing Salve

8 oz. Cold-Pressed Organic Coconut Oil

1 oz. Beeswax

2 drops Vitamin E (optional)

10 drops Lavender Essential Oil

5 drops Myrrh Essential Oil

3 drops Helichrysum Essential Oil

Glass Jars or Tin Containers

Place the coconut oil and beeswax over a double-boiler, and gently warm over low heat until the beeswax melts. Remove from heat and add the essential oils and Vitamin E oil, (if using). Quickly pour the mixture into glass jars or tins, and allow to cool completely. Store salve in a cool location where they will not re-melt and re-solidify. When stored correctly, salve will last for 1-3 years. Yields 8 oz.

SAFETY PRECAUTIONS

To prevent chemical burns and poisonings, keep chemicals and cleaning products safely stored away from pets. The following is a list of safety recommendations for the use of chemicals and dangerous substances:

• Use chemicals in a well-ventilated area.

• Keep chemicals in their original containers which provide the exact ingredients and instructions in case of accidental ingestion or exposure.

• Avoid using chemicals.

• Do not mix chemicals.

• Do not use or store chemicals near food or drinks.

• Safely confine your pet away from chemicals while in use.

• Wear recommended protection such as gloves or goggles, safety goggles when using chemicals.

In the event a chemical is ingested, do not induce vomiting. **Call Animal Poison Control* Immediately.**

*Animal Poison Control Hotline : 1-800-548-2423

CANCER

Our pets are living longer lives due to better nutrition, preventative care and advances in medicine. Cancer is largely a disease of older pets, and the prevalence of cancer is rising. Any lump, bump or growth should be evaluated by your veterinarian. Pet owners commonly discover such changes in their pets simply by petting, brushing and bathing them.

Tumors and cancer develop because of an abnormal change in the cell's DNA. Some of these changes may be genetic (due to family history), yet many are random. Several other factors have been suggested to play a role in the development of cancer, such as the environment, poor diet and infectious agents. Cancers affecting younger pets may be attributed to breed-associated links or viruses such as feline leukemia virus (FeLV), feline immunodeficiency virus (FIV) and canine papilloma virus.

One of the primary reasons to spay or neuter your pet is to reduce or nearly eliminate the risk of mammary gland cancer in females and testicular cancer in males. When these procedures are performed at a young age (6 months old and prior to any estrus cycles in females), the risk of these cancers is greatly decreased.

Choosing if and how to treat your pet's cancer is a personal decision involving several considerations such as the type of cancer, prognosis, quality of life, estimated time of survival, and finances. Traditional treatment options for pets include surgery, chemotherapy, and radiation, similar to our own choices for cancer therapy.

Essential oils may be used in conjunction with traditional cancer treatments or instead of aggressive or invasive methods of cancer treatment. Essential oils support your pet's immune system, aid digestion, increase appetite, and improve energy and well-being.

Many essential oils have the capabilities of affecting cancer cells. Frankincense, in particular, has been shown to kill cancer cells in animal laboratory studies. Citrus oils contain a natural chemical of particular importance in cancer prevention called d-limonene. In fact, the essential oils of grapefruit, tangerine, and orange contain over 90 percent d-limonene. This simple compound has been found in nearly 100 studies in animals and in humans to prevent cancer and stop the progression of cancer. It has been shown to be active against several types of tumor cells, including mammary, skin, lung, liver and forestomach in rodents as well as colon and breast cancer cells in humans.

> *"Sometimes you don't need words to feel better; you just need the nearness of your dog."*
>
> *- Natalie Lloyd*

For dogs, apply Frankincense, Sandalwood, Geranium, Lavender and Myrrh daily. Apply daily, Grounding Blend for calming and Digestive Blend for digestive upset or to increase appetite. Apply Soothing Blend daily for pain relief. Add Grapefruit or Lemon essential oil to the drinking water if there are no cats in the home. Diffuse Protective Blend, Frankincense, and Lemon or Grapefruit to support well-being and purify the air and uplift the mood. Apply Calming Blend to yourself and your pet, and diffuse it to promote a feeling of calm during this stressful time.

For cats, apply Frankincense, Sandalwood, Geranium, Lavender and Myrrh daily. Apply Soothing Blend daily for pain relief. Add Digestive Blend and/or Lavender to the litter box as described in Litter Box Power to support healthy digestion and ease anxiety. Diffuse Protective Blend, Frankincense, and Lemon or Grapefruit to support well-being and purify the air and uplift the mood. Apply Calming Blend to yourself and your pet, and diffuse it to promote a feeling of calm during this stressful time.

Additional steps you can take if your pet has cancer and they are just good general practice. Convert to natural cleaners and air-fresheners, remove toxins, switch to natural grooming products, use natural or unscented cat litter, and feed a diet free from preservatives and chemicals. Support your pet by feeding a high quality diet and supplement Omega-3 and probiotics.

Orange

FOR DOGS

Apply 1 drop each Frankincense, Sandalwood, Geranium, Lavender and Myrrh 2-3 times daily.

Apply 1-2 drops Digestive Blend 2-3 times daily or as needed.

Apply 1-2 drops Soothing Blend 2-3 times daily or as needed.

Apply 1-2 drops Grounding Blend or Calming Blend as needed.

Add 1 drop Grapefruit or Lemon oil to 2 cups drinking water (if there are no cats in the home).

Diffuse Protective Blend, Frankincense, and Lemon or Grapefruit, for 20-30 minutes 2-3 times daily.

Diffuse Calming Blend for 20-30 minutes for 2-3 times daily.

FOR CATS

Apply 1 drop each Frankincense, Sandalwood, Geranium, Lavender and Myrrh 2-3 times daily.

Apply 1-2 drops Digestive Blend 2-3 times daily or as needed.

Dilute 1 drop Soothing Blend in 4 Tbsp. carrier oil and apply 1 drop 2-3 times daily or as needed.

Apply 1-2 drops Grounding Blend or Calming Blend as needed.

Diffuse Protective Blend, Frankincense, and Lemon or Grapefruit, for 20-30 minutes 2-3 times daily.

Diffuse Calming Blend for 20-30 minutes for 2-3 times daily.

CANINE COGNITIVE DISORDER

Elderly pets may develop "old dog dementia" termed Canine Cognitive Disorder or CCD. A pet suffering from CCD may seem lost or confused, even in familiar surroundings. Additional signs include inability to sleep, pacing or wandering, and staring aimlessly. Dogs afflicted with CCD affect the entire household by disrupting sleep, having accidents indoors, and frustrating their loving family.

Pets have a very sensitive sense of smell, and smell has been closely linked with memory, probably more so than any of the other senses. A combination of essential oil blends and single oils may be helpful for CCD by triggering memory and may safely be used to complement traditional therapy without side effects or interactions. Calming Blend is perfect for inducing sleep and restfulness. Grounding Blend is useful for reducing stress and anxiety. The third component of essential oil therapy for CCD is Frankincense. Frankincense is considered the life force oil and is helpful for many neurologic disorders. Two other single oils which may be affective are Wild Orange and Lavender. By using essential oils, within a short period of time, your pet and the whole family should feel more at ease.

Maintaining a predictable routine, feeding a healthy diet and supplementing with higher quantities of antioxidants, Omega 3 fatty acids, l-carnitine and SAMe are all important for stability in CCD patients.

FOR DOGS

Option 1: Apply 1-2 drops of Grounding Blend and Frankincense 2 or more times daily. Apply 1-2 drops and/ or diffuse Calming Blend in the evening.

Option 2: Apply 1-2 drops of Grounding Blend and Frankincense 2 or more times daily. Apply or diffuse equal parts Wild Orange and Lavender in the evening.

In addition to high quality nutrition and essential oils, several supplements have shown improvement in signs of CCD. Supplement with higher quantities of antioxidants, Omega 3 fatty acids, l-carnitine and SAMe.

CHEWING

Although it is normal for puppies to chew, they can quickly damage your furniture, home, and belongings. Chewing is a normal part of a puppy's emotional development and the development of their jaws and teeth. Puppies, like infants and toddlers, explore their world by putting objects into their mouths. Puppies may teethe for 6-8 months, which can create some oral discomfort. Chewing not only facilitates teething, but also helps gums feel better.

As adults, chewing is relaxing, enjoyable and serves a physical need. However, adult dogs should understand what is permissible and what is not permissible to chew. As a puppy, he or she may not have been clearly taught what to chew and what not to chew.

Adult dogs may engage in destructive chewing for a number of reasons. In order to deal with this behavior, you must first determine the cause(s). Possible reasons for destructive chewing include:

Boredom

Separation anxiety

Fear-related behavior

Attention-seeking behavior

Lack of proper training

(See Anxiety and Stress)

Important! You may need to consult a behavior professional for help with both separation anxiety and fear-related behaviors. Most puppies and dogs benefit from training classes or the help of a private trainer or behaviorist. Discuss your concerns with your veterinarian.

To deter chewing behavior, apply diluted Cassia (a hot oil), Black Pepper (a hot oil) or citrus oils to the locations and things your puppy or dog likes to chew. If chewing continues, increase the amount of essential oils applied.

FOR DOGS

Chew Deterrent Spray with Essential Oils

Add 5-6 drops of Cassia, Black Pepper, or citrus essential oil to a 4 oz. glass spray bottle and fill with water. Shake the bottle well to mix. Test the spray on a hidden area of your furniture (or other object which your puppy/dog likes to chew) to ensure it will not stain or mark the item. Spray generously and reapply as the smell wears off. If the spray does not seem to be working well, add more of the essential oil or prepare the Chew Deterrent Spray with a different hot essential oil.

CONSTIPATION

Constipation in pets is usually due to a poor diet. Obesity increases your pet's risk of constipation.

Feeding your pet a healthy diet, increasing fiber intake and hydration and supplementing with a probiotic can help to decrease constipation.

A high quality diet is vitally important. If the pet food is dry, consider adding warm water to the food to soften it and add moisture. Add fiber in the form of psyllium powder, fruits and vegetables (avoid grapes, raisins, garlic and onions). A daily probiotic powder or capsule will support a healthy digestive system and immune system.

Essential oils are a natural way to restore normal bowel function. The best way to apply essential oils for constipation is to massage your pet's lower abdomen with Digestive Blend daily. If the condition persists for more than one day, add Myrrh and Lavender to your daily regimen. Research has shown that stress can affect how the digestive system functions and can cause constipation. Keeping your pet calm will help them to feel more comfortable. Diffuse Calming Blend or Lavender daily.

Do not give your pet any over the counter constipation medication or mineral oil. If the condition persists for more than 2-3 days, see your veterinarian. Your veterinarian may recommend a special diet.

FOR DOGS

Apply 1-2 drops of Digestive Blend topically up to 4 times daily. If possible, apply and massage the oil into your pet's lower abdomen for 5-7 minutes.

If the condition persists for more than 1 day, apply 1-2 drops each Digestive Blend, Lavender and Myrrh up to 4 times daily and massage the oils into the lower abdomen for 5-7 minutes.

Diffuse Calming Blend or Lavender for 20-30 minutes 2-3 times daily.

Feed your pet a high quality food. Add water and fiber to your pet's food (avoid grapes, raisins, garlic and onions).

If the condition persists for more than 2-3 days, call your veterinarian.

FOR CATS

Apply 1 drop Digestive Blend 1-2 times daily and massage the abdomen for 5 minutes.

If the condition persists, apply 1-2 drops each Digestive Blend, Lavender and Myrrh up to 4 times daily and massage the oils into the lower abdomen for 5-7 minutes.

Add Digestive Blend to the litter box as described in Litter Box Power.

Diffuse Calming Blend or Lavender for 20-30 minutes 2-3 times daily.

Feed your pet a high quality food. Add water and fiber to your pet's food (avoid grapes, raisins, garlic and onions).

If the condition persists for more than 2-3 days, call your veterinarian.

COPROPHAGIA

Coprophagia is the act of dog's eating feces. It is truly disgusting, and and it is not really understood. Dogs eat feces, usually their own, for several reasons. One common explanation is a dietary deficiency, yet our pets are so spoiled and well fed, that a missing nutrient is hard to imagine. Often, a puppy who has had an accident is trying to avoid getting caught. Another explanation is that this awful behavior has become a habit for the dog. A habit can develop from boredom, lack of stimulation and activity, or stress and anxiety.

" There is no psychiatrist in the world like a puppy licking your face."

- Ben Williams

First, be sure to feed a high quality diet and supplement with omega-3 and probiotics. Further support good digestion with Digestive Blend applied twice daily. Diffuse citrus oils to reduce stress and anxiety.

Ensure your dog is getting adequate exercise, mental stimulation and attention. Discuss this condition with your veterinarian and trainer.

FOR DOGS

Apply 1-2 drops of Digestive Blend twice daily.

Diffuse Citrus oils for 20-30 minutes 2-3 times daily.

Feed a healthy diet and supplement with omega-3 and probiotics.

CUTS AND SCRAPES

Active, curious pets often get into trouble or have small accidents. Minor cuts can happen very easily. Examples include cutting toe pads, slipping on the ice, stepping on rocks outside, and broken toenails. Contact your veterinarian, if the cut is actively bleeding, will not stop bleeding or is deeper than the surface of the skin or if your pet is limping due to the injury, continues to lick at a wound for more than 1-2 days. We do not advise bandaging wounds without the recommendation of your veterinarian.

The basic steps for treating a minor cut or scrape are:
- Stop the bleeding. Apply pressure if necessary.
- Clean the wound. Remove any foreign material. (If the wound is deep, contact your veterinarian.)
- Apply an antibiotic essential oil.
- Keep the wound clean and dry.
- Monitor for signs of infection such as a yellow or green discharge.

Essential oils are ideal choices for any of these steps because they have cleansing, antibacterial and pain relieving properties. In addition, they are calming for both you and your pet in this stressful situation.

In the event of a minor, superficial wound, first stop the bleeding. Many times, applying pressure for a few minutes is effective. If additional help is needed, apply Helichrysum or Lemon (not in cats) to aid in blood clotting.

• After the bleeding has stopped, immediately clean the wound with Gentle Cleanser (See recipe) or hydrogen peroxide using gauze or cotton balls. Hydrogen peroxide is an effective cleanser initially, but it is best to use it only once. Repeated use of hydrogen peroxide can delay healing. Continue cleaning the wound with Gentle Cleanser 1-2 times daily.

• Apply 1-2 drops Lavender essential oil. Lavender is a natural antiseptic and pain reliever. Lavender may briefly sting, but after a few seconds, the sting disappears and the sensation changes to relief. Simultaneously, the aroma of Lavender is calming. After applying Lavender directly to the wound, rub 2-3 drops in the palms of your hands, and let your pet inhale the soothing fragrance.

• Several other essential oils that have antibacterial properties including Frankincense, Myrrh, and Melaleuca (diluted in cats) can be used. Apply 1-2 drops of each Lavender, Frankincense or Myrrh and Melaleuca (dilute in cats) to the wound to prevent infection. Repeat the application of the antibacterial essential oil every 4-6 hours for the first 3 days. After that time, the risk of infection is greatly reduced. After 3 days, continue to apply the antibacterial essential oils 1-2 times daily.

• Beginning on day 4, apply Helichrysum daily during the healing process to reduce or eliminate scarring.

• Keep the wound clean and dry, and protect it by restricting your pet's time outdoors.

• For several days, continue to diffuse Calming Blend or Lavender alternating with Protective Blend to help calm the household and reduce the risk of infection. Add Lavender to the litter box as described in Litter Box Power.

• Continue high quality nutrition and supplements with Omega-3 and Probiotics.

FOR DOGS

Stop the bleeding with pressure for 3-5 minutes. If bleeding does not subside, apply 1 drop Helichrysum or Lemon. **If bleeding persists, call your veterinarian.**

Clean the wound with Gentle Cleanser or Hydrogen peroxide initially. Clean with Gentle Cleanser daily during the healing process.

Apply 1-2 drops each Lavender, Frankincense or Myrrh and Melaleuca every 4-6 hours for the first 3 days. After 3 days, continue to apply the above oils 1-2 times daily.

Beginning on day 4, apply Helichrysum daily.

Diffuse Calming Blend or Lavender for 20-30 minutes twice daily.

Diffuse Protective Blend for 20-30 minutes twice daily.

Continue high quality nutrition and supplements with Omega-3 and probiotics.

FOR CATS

Stop the bleeding with pressure for 3-5 minutes. If bleeding does not subside, apply 1 drop Helichrysum. **If bleeding persists, call your veterinarian.**

Clean the wound with Gentle Cleanser or Hydrogen peroxide initially. Clean with Gentle Cleanser daily during the healing process.

Apply 1 drop each Lavender, Frankincense or Myrrh repeat every 4-6 hours.

Dilute 1 drop Melaleuca in 4 Tbsp. of carrier oil, apply 1-2 times daily.

Diffuse Calming Blend or Lavender for 20-30 minutes twice daily.

Diffuse Protective Blend for 20 30 minutes twice daily.

Add Lavender to the litter box as described in Litter Box Power.

Continue high quality nutrition and supplement with Omega-3 and Probiotics.

Gentle Cleanser

4 ounces Castile soap or unscented natural foaming soap

2 drops Roman Chamomile Essential Oil

2 drops Lavender Essential Oil

DEMODEX/MANGE

Demodectic Mange, referred to as Demodex, is a mite infestation commonly seen in puppies, young adults, and old dogs. Demodectic mites live in the hair follicles and are not contagious to people. Demodex is often associated with a suppressed immune system.

Signs of demodex include patches of hair loss, redness of the skin and crusty eruptions of the skin. Some dogs are itchy when they have this condition. Your veterinarian will diagnose demodex with a physical and microscopic exam. Demodex may be treated with oral or topical medication and medicated shampoo. Complete cure may take weeks to months.

Essential oils complement traditional therapy. Apply Lavender, Melaleuca, Cleansing Blend and Helichrysum daily to the affected areas or by petting. Apply Healing Salve daily (See recipe). Bathe weekly to twice weekly with Antiseptic Shampoo (See recipe) with 2 drops Cleansing Blend added. Feed your pet a high quality diet and supplement with Omega-3 and probiotics.

FOR DOGS

Apply 1 drop each of Cleansing Blend, Melaleuca, Lavender, and Helichrysum to affected areas or by petting twice daily.

Apply Healing Salve 1-2 times daily to localized lesions.

Bathe with Soothing Skin Shampoo with added Cleansing Blend 1-2 times weekly.

Feed a high quality diet and supplement with Omega-3 and probiotics.

Antiseptic Shampoo

10 oz. Water

2 oz. Aloe Vera

1 Tbsp. of Castile soap

2 drops of Myrrh Essential Oil

2 drops of Lavender Essential Oil

2 drops of Melaleuca Essential Oil

2 drops Cleansing Essential Oil Blend

Combine in a jar. Shake well. Lather and rinse well.

Healing Salve

8 oz. Cold-Pressed Organic Coconut Oil

1 oz. Beeswax

2 drops Vitamin E (optional)

10 drops Lavender Essential Oil

5 drops Myrrh Essential Oil

3 drops Helichrysum Essential Oil

Glass Jars or Tin Containers

Place the coconut oil and beeswax over a double-boiler, and gently warm over low heat until the beeswax melts. Remove from heat and add the essential oils and Vitamin E oil, (if using). Quickly pour the mixture into glass jars or tins, and allow to cool completely. Store salve in a cool location where they will not re-melt and re-solidify. When stored correctly, salve will last for 1-3 years. Yields 8 oz.

DENTAL CARE

Dental disease affects the entire body. Caring for your pet's teeth and gums improves the quality of their life and extends it. Bacteria that accumulate in the mouth enter the bloodstream and can adversely affect the kidneys, heart and liver. Dental disease also causes terrible oral pain, bad breath and possible difficulty eating or chewing properly. Once a pet's teeth and gums are severely infected, receded or diseased (periodontal disease), extractions will most likely be needed.

In addition to oral examinations with each veterinary visit, dogs and cats should have annual dental cleanings, much like our own, in order to maintain healthy teeth and gums. Performing routine veterinary examinations, regular dental cleanings and good home care will prevent the progression of periodontal disease.

"Dogs are not our whole life, but they make our lives whole."

- Roger Caras

Home care is very important. It is ideal to brush your pet's teeth daily with fluoride-free toothpaste. Toothpastes made for pets are available in flavors such as beef, peanut butter and fish. Brushing may be difficult for some dogs and for most cats to accept. So, the next best option is to offer safe and effective dental chews daily. Avoid giving your dog real bones as they can fracture teeth, splinter or become lodged in their mouth or throat. A third option is to put a veterinary dental water additive in the drinking water to delay tartar accumulation. Any of these three methods of home dental care may be combined.

Don't be discouraged if tartar still builds up on your pet's teeth. There is nothing that will prevent tartar 100%. Even with the best home care, your pet will still benefit from dental cleanings on an annual basis.

Essential oils can help maintain a strong immune system, fight bacteria and reduce pain. For dogs and cats, apply Myrrh and Helichrysum once to twice daily. Add Protective Blend or Lemon to drinking water for dogs (if there are no cats in the home). Diffuse Protective Blend and Lemon, alternating oils every few days.

FOR DOGS

Apply 1 drop Myrrh and 1 drop Helichrysum 1-2 times daily.

Add 1 drop Protective Blend or 1 drop Lemon to 2 cups drinking water (if there are no cats in the home).

Diffuse Protective Blend or Lemon, alternating oils every few days.

FOR CATS

Apply 1 drop Myrrh and 1 drop Helichrysum 1-2 times daily.

Diffuse Protective Blend or Lemon, alternating oils every few days.

Note: Do not add essential oils to the drinking water in a home with cats.

DIABETES

Diabetes mellitus is a disease in which blood sugar levels are abnormally high. Diabetes is characterized by a lack of production of insulin by the pancreas or the body's resistance or inability to use insulin. Insulin is a hormone that regulates blood sugar levels. When blood sugar levels rise, such as after a meal, the pancreas secretes insulin to reduce the blood sugar and enable the cells to utilize the sugar for energy.

Causes of diabetes in dogs include heredity, infection, obesity, and pancreatitis. In cats, potential causes of diabetes include obesity and protein accumulation in the cells of the pancreas.

Common signs of diabetes are excessive thirst, excessive urination, increased appetite, and weight loss. Diabetic pets are also susceptible to increased infections and may have difficulty healing.

Cinnamon, found in a metabolic blend

In addition to insulin therapy guided by your veterinarian, several essential oils are helpful to regulate blood sugar, improve metabolism, slow the absorption of carbohydrates and heal secondary infections. The use of essential oils in diabetes may reduce or eliminate the amount of insulin needed.

The essential oils in the Metabolic Blend include Grapefruit, Lemon, Peppermint, Ginger and Cinnamon. These essential oils help to regulate blood sugar and promote a healthy metabolism. Apply Metabolic Blend daily (diluted for cats). Add Metabolic Blend to the drinking water for dogs (if there are no cats in the home). Apply or diffuse Grounding Blend or Calming Blend twice daily to reduce anxiety and stress. Continue to supplement with Omega-3 and probiotics.

FOR DOGS

Apply 1-2 drops Metabolic Blend 2-3 times daily.

Add 1 drop of Metabolic Blend to 2 cups drinking water (if there are no cats in the home).

Apply 1 drop Grounding Blend or Calming Blend twice daily.

Diffuse Grounding Blend or Calming Blend for 20-30 minutes 2-3 times daily.

Continue to supplement with Omega-3 and probiotics.

FOR CATS

Dilute 1 drop Metabolic Blend in 4 Tbsp. of carrier oil and apply twice daily.

Apply 1 drop Grounding Blend or Calming Blend twice daily.

Diffuse Grounding Blend or Calming Blend for 20-30 minutes 2-3 times daily.

Continue to supplement with Omega-3 and probiotics.

DIARRHEA AND VOMITING

Diarrhea and vomiting may have a number of causes. Most commonly, dogs and cats encounter short-lived viruses, stomach bugs or intestinal parasites (See Intestinal Parasites). Dogs may chew on leaves or grass outside, resulting in mild diarrhea, gas or an upset stomach. Occasionally, pets misbehave by getting into the garbage. Table food may also upset the digestive system.

Often, pets do not tolerate abrupt changes in diet. When changing your pet's brand of food, flavor or formula, introduce the new food gradually over 5-7 days to ease the transition and avoid diarrhea and vomiting.

Stress also can cause stomach upset. What causes feelings of stress in our pets? New situations, moving, large gatherings, guests in the home, a new baby, changes in work schedules and traveling are all examples of stressful instances. (See Stress and Anxiety) Under these circumstances, Digestive Blend and Myrrh are quite helpful.

For Dogs, apply Digestive Blend and Myrrh topically to your dog several times daily to reduce symptoms. Rub the oil on your pet's belly or anywhere on the body. It will be absorbed and work even if it is applied to the back. Diffuse Protective Blend to support the immune system.

For cats, place Digestive Blend and Myrrh in the palm of your hands and rub your hands together to allow most of the oil to absorb. Apply by petting your cat daily or as needed. Rub the oil on your pet's belly or anywhere on the body and it will be absorbed and work even if it is applied to the back. Diffuse Protective Blend to support the immune system.

For both dogs and cats, withhold food initially for 12-24 hours, then offer a bland diet of boiled chicken, low fat chopped meat, rice, cottage cheese and yogurt. Continue the bland diet in smaller, more frequent meals until signs of diarrhea or vomiting have passed for at least three days. Then, gradually convert back to your pet's healthy, regular diet. Once vomiting has ceased, continue to administer your pet's probiotic. If your pet refuses the bland diet or vomits everything he or she eats or drinks, contact your veterinarian.

In all cases of diarrhea and vomiting, your pet is losing important fluids. It is very important to maintain proper hydration to allow all the organs of the body to function well. Offer your pet water and add additional water to the homemade rice. If your pet is not eating and drinking well or has suffered several days of vomiting or diarrhea, dehydration may need to be treated by your veterinarian.

A word of caution: If diarrhea or vomiting persists for more than 1-2 days, increases in frequency or is bloody, call your veterinarian. Severe lethargy and lack of appetite are also indications that you should contact your veterinarian. If there is any possibility that your pet may have eaten an indigestible object such as a toy, clothing, or string, seek veterinary care immediately. Several days of illness may be due to a more severe condition such as intestinal parasites, kidney or liver disease, or other metabolic disease.

FOR DOGS

Apply 1-2 drops each Digestive Blend and Myrrh 4-6 times daily as needed.

Diffuse Protective Blend for 20-30 minutes 2-3 times daily.

FOR CATS

Apply 1 drop Digestive Blend and 1 drop Myrrh 1-2 times daily.

Diffuse Protective Blend for 20-30 minutes 2-3 times daily.

Fennel, found in a digestive blend

FOR DOGS & CATS

Withhold food initially for 12-24 hours, then offer a bland diet of boiled chicken, low fat chopped meat, rice, cottage cheese and yogurt. Continue the bland diet in smaller, more frequent meals until signs of diarrhea or vomiting have passed for at least three days. Then, gradually convert back to your pet's healthy, regular diet.

Once vomiting has ceased, continue to administer the probiotic.

A Word of Caution: If diarrhea or vomiting persists for more than 1-2 days, increases in frequency or is bloody, call your veterinarian. Severe lethargy and lack of appetite are also indications to contact your veterinarian.

DRY SKIN (SEBORRHEA SICCA)

Skin stays moist due to the production of sebum (oil). Dry skin occurs when the skin does not naturally produce enough sebum. Pets commonly develop dry, flaky skin in the winter months or from over bathing. Fortunately, there are a number of essential oils that help to stimulate the production of sebum and also balance secretions within the skin, thus helping dry skin.

Essential oils are both calming and gentle and help to soothe dry, itchy, and inflamed skin. Bathe your dog 1-2 times weekly with a natural shampoo adding Lavender, Roman Chamomile, and Myrrh essential oils to help soothe, calm, and repair the skin (See Soothing Skin Shampoo recipe). Apply Lavender, Sandalwood, and Roman Chamomile daily. Be sure to feed your dog a high quality diet and supplement with Omega-3 and a probiotic. Cats generally do not tolerate bathing. For cats who have dry skin, we suggest applying Lavender, Sandalwood, and Roman Chamomile daily. Be sure to feed your cat a high quality diet and supplement with Omega-3 and a probiotic.

FOR DOGS

Bathe 1-2 times weekly using Soothing Skin Shampoo with Lavender, Myrrh and Roman Chamomile added (See recipe). Caution: When bathing with essential oils, be careful to avoid the eyes.

Dilute 1-2 drops each of Lavender, Sandalwood and Roman Chamomile in 2-4 Tbsp. of carrier oil and apply 1-2 times daily. When working with a carrier oil, make sure to rub the oil onto your dog very well, so as not to stain carpeting or furniture.

Feed a high quality diet and supplement with Omega-3 and probiotics.

FOR CATS

We recommend you find a groomer that specializes in cats and have your groomer use the Soothing Skin Shampoo with Lavender, Myrrh and Roman Chamomile added (See recipe below).

Dilute 1-2 drops each of Lavender, Sandalwood and Roman Chamomile in 2-4 Tbsp. of carrier oil and apply 1-2 times daily. When working with a carrier oil, make sure to rub it onto your cat very well, so as not to stain carpeting or furniture.

Feed a high quality diet and supplement with Omega-3 and probiotics.

Soothing Skin Shampoo

3 oz. Castile soap (available at many health and bulk food stores)

2 oz. Organic unpasteurized, unfiltered apple cider vinegar

1 oz. Vegetable Glycerin

2 oz. Distilled water

3 drops Lavender Essential Oil

3 drops Roman Chamomile Essential Oil

3 drops Myrrh Essential Oil

Optional: add 1 tsp. ground oatmeal

EAR CLEANING

The first step in becoming comfortable in cleaning our pets' ears is to understand their anatomy. A dog or cat's ear canal is a long, "L" shaped tube in which the ear drum is protected by being a distance from the surface. It has a vertical canal, nearly a 90 degree turn, and a horizontal canal prior to reaching the ear drum (tympanic membrane). It is quite different from our ear canal, which is short, and straight, and easy to touch. Since your pet's ear drum is literally inches away and past a curve, it is protected.

However, the shape of the ear canal makes dogs and cats predisposed to ear infections. The ear canal is naturally deep and dark, so any moisture (humidity, bathing, swimming, etc.) can easily contribute to an infection. The goal of cleaning your pet's ears is to maintain a dry environment that discourages the growth of bacteria and yeast. The process of cleaning your pet's ears when it is infected or maintaining a healthy ear canal is the same. The only difference is in the frequency of cleaning the ears.

Generously apply 1-3 tsp. of a safe ear cleaner as directed by your veterinarian and massage the ear canal. A natural ear cleaner recipe is listed below. Either pour the cleaner into the ear canal and massage, or saturate a cotton ball, place it at the top of the ear canal, and massage the ear to release the fluid. Remove the cotton ball. Proceed with wiping out the ear canal with dry cotton balls. (The cotton ball method is useful for cats.)

You will know that a sufficient amount of cleaner has been applied when a swishing sound can be heard as you massage the ear canal, loosening debris and driving it to the surface. Using cotton balls, wipe the ear canal by inserting your finger as deeply as you can. Although this sounds aggressive, your finger cannot reach the ear drum. Continue to flush the ear with cleaning solution and wipe with cotton balls until the canal is clean and the cotton balls are removed with very little or no debris.

After having an ear cleaning, pets will often rub their heads on the floor, rub against the furniture and shake their heads excessively. Do not worry that you have done any harm. The ears simply feel wet and different to your pet.

Note: To clean your pet's ears, you may need the support of a second person, especially for cats. Confine your pet to a small room, and make the experience as positive as possible. Treats as enticement and reward are helpful.

For cats, you may only be able to wipe 2 or 3 times. That's OK. It is better to keep the atmosphere positive for a short cleaning than to struggle for quite some time.

We generally recommend cleaning weekly to every two weeks based on seasonal humidity and contact with water. During an infection, the frequency of cleaning is often increased to three times weekly. Apply Lavender essential oil around the base of the ear to help calm your pet and prevent infection.

Signs of an ear infection include scratching at the ear(s), shaking his or her head, holding the head to one side, redness, inflammation, debris in the ears and an unpleasant odor from the ear(s). If your pet demonstrates severe signs of discomfort or if signs of an infection persist, contact your veterinarian.

FOR DOGS & CATS

Clean ears with Natural Ear Cleaner (See recipe) every 1-2 weeks for maintenance or up to three times weekly for treatment of an infection.

Apply Lavender around (not in the ear canal) the base of the ears.

Witch Hazel

Natural Ear Cleaner

1 oz. Witch Hazel

1 oz. Apple Cider Vinegar

Sometimes referred to as nature's antibiotic ointment, witch hazel can be effective in cleaning your pet's ears while protecting them from further infection. This natural remedy, produced from the leaves and bark of the North American witch hazel shrub, encourages quicker healing of minor breaks in skin and has proven anti-inflammatory properties.

Used for decades in folk medicine, apple cider vinegar has been proven to kill germs and heal naturally.

EAR INFECTIONS

Dogs and cats are particularly susceptible to ear infections due to their long, deep and curved ear canals. The dark environment coupled with moisture, due to bathing, swimming, humidity, rain, etc., provide the perfect environment for yeast and bacteria to grow. Ear infections may be prevented by properly cleaning your pet's ears regularly, and especially after contact with water (See Ear Cleaning). A dog or cat may also be likely to develop ear infections as a result of allergies (seasonal, food or contact), some medical conditions and as members of certain breeds (See Allergies).

> *" As every cat owner knows,*
> *nobody owns a cat."*
>
> *- Ellen Perry Berkeley*

At the first sign of redness, irritation, scratching or rubbing of the ears, clean your pet's ears (See Ear Cleaning).

Essential oils applied around the base of the ear can help treat an ear infection and/or prevent an infection. Never pour essential oils directly into the ear canal. Lavender, Geranium, Frankincense and Melaleuca are all essential oils that kill infection-causing bacteria and yeast and can help to ease any discomfort your pet may be feeling as a result of an ear infection.

FOR DOGS

Apply 1-2 drops of Geranium, Lavender, Frankincense, and Melaleuca around the base of the ear-front and back, on the outside only, 2-3 times daily.

Diffuse Protective Blend for 20-30 minutes 2-3 times daily.

Support the immune system with a healthy diet and a probiotic.

FOR CATS

Apply 1-2 drops of Geranium, Lavender, and Frankincense, around the base of the ear-front and back, on the outside only, 2-3 times daily.

Diffuse Protective Blend for 20-30 minutes 2-3 times daily.

Support the immune system with a healthy diet and a probiotic.

EAR MITES

Ear Mites in cats are parasites that live only in the ear canals and are highly contagious between cats. Ear mites are diagnosed with a microscopic exam performed by your veterinarian. Most commonly, ear mites cause black debris in the ears and cause scratching and irritation. Lavender, Cleansing Blend, and Rosemary are a good complement to traditional treatment and are beneficial in helping to eliminate ear mites. Essential oils reduce itching and relieve irritation in the ear.

FOR CATS

Clean your cat's ears weekly (See Ear Cleaning).

Mix 1 drop each of Lavender, Cleansing Blend and Rosemary in 4 Tbsp. of carrier oil and apply the mixture daily around the base of your cat's ears. Also apply the mixture at the very top of the ear canals daily using a cotton swab.

Note: When using essential oils for cats or for any condition which persists or worsens, contact your veterinarian.

"Time spent with cats is never wasted."

-*Sigmund Freud*

FELINE ACNE

Cats often develop acne on their chins and around their lips. Often this is due to plastic bowls or toys, food allergies and contact allergies to chemicals such as cleaning products. First, change to stainless steel, glass or ceramic bowls and switch to natural cleaning products. Wash your cat's chin daily with a gentle natural soap and apply Lavender and/or Myrrh essential oils and Healing Salve daily (See recipe). If the breakouts persist, consider changing your cat's diet (See Nutrition) and see your veterinarian.

FOR CATS

Wash your cat's chin daily with a gentle, natural soap (See recipe for Gentle Cleanser).

Dilute 1 drop Lavender and or Myrrh in 4 Tbsp. of Carrier oil and apply to affected area daily.

Healing Salve

Healing Salve
8 oz. Cold-Pressed Organic Coconut Oil
1 oz Beeswax
2 drops Vitamin E (optional)
10 drops Lavender
5 drops Myrrh
3 drops Helichrysum
Glass Jars or Tin Containers

Place the coconut oil and beeswax over a double –boiler, and gently warm over low heat until the beeswax melts. Remove from heat and add the essential oils and Vitamin E oil, (if using). Quickly pour the mixture into glass jars or tins, and allow to cool completely. Store salve in a cool location where they will not re-melt and re-solidify. When stored correctly, salve will last for 1-3 years. Yields 8 ounces.

Gentle Cleanser

4 oz. Castile soap or unscented natural foaming soap
2 drops Roman Chamomile Essential Oil
2 drops Lavender Essential Oil

FLEAS, TICKS AND MOSQUITOES

Fleas, ticks and mosquitoes carry a number of diseases and parasites. Some of these are not only dangerous to your pet, but also to you and your family. The most common consequences of flea, tick and mosquito bites include Heartworm disease (from mosquitoes), Hemobartonellosis/Cat Scratch Fever (from fleas and ticks), Tapeworms (from fleas) and Lyme disease (from ticks). (See specific sections for more details).

These parasites are present across much of the United States and are found in many different environments and climates. Fleas, ticks and mosquitoes can survive all year round, despite changes in the seasons.

Fleas, in particular, can be very difficult to rid from the home. Thus, prevention is the best way to avoid the possible consequences of fleas, ticks and mosquitoes. Eucalyptus essential oil or Repellent Blend repels insects, fleas, and ticks effectively for several hours. Pure essential oils are perfectly safe for you, your children and your pets.

If fleas or ticks have invaded your home, a combination approach is most effective. Treat your home with a natural flea bomb (See Natural Flea Bomb recipe). Clean your home with Protective Blend Cleaner concentrate, launder bedding with Protective Blend laundry detergent and diffuse Cleansing Blend or Protective Blend in your home. Bathe pets with a natural shampoo effective against pests (See Flea & Tick Repellent Shampoo or Spray).

FOR DOGS & CATS

Fleas: For prevention, dilute Repellent Blend 1:1 with water in a glass spray bottle. Apply by spraying your pet's entire body 2-3 times daily. Be careful to avoid the eyes. See below for Do-It-Yourself Homemade Flea Collar and Flea Repellant Spray and Shampoo.

If fleas have invaded your home, a combination approach is most effective.

Treat your home with a natural flea bomb (See Natural Flea Bomb recipe).

Clean your home with Protective Blend Cleaner Concentrate.

Launder bedding with Protective Blend laundry detergent.

Diffuse Cleansing Blend or Protective Blend in your home.

Bathe pets with a natural shampoo effective against pests (See Flea & Tick Repellent Shampoo or Spray).

Continue these steps to prevent pests all year round.

FOR DOGS & CATS

Ticks: For prevention dilute 1:1 Cleansing Blend, Protective Blend or Repellent Blend with water in a glass spray bottle and spray your pet. Apply by spraying your pet's entire body 2-3 times daily. Be careful to avoid the eyes. See below for Do-It-Yourself Flea and Tick Repellant Spray and Shampoo.

Continue these steps to prevent pests all year round.

FOR DOGS

Flea, Mosquito, and Tick Bites: Apply 1 drop each Lavender and Melaleuca directly to Mosquito or flea bites 3-4 times daily for as long as needed.

FOR CATS

Flea, Mosquito, and Tick Bites: Apply 1 drop each Lavender and Myrrh directly to Mosquito or flea bites 3-4 times daily for as long as needed.

Flea & Tick Repellent Shampoo or Spray

Add the following to 8 oz. of all natural shampoo base:

4 drops Clary Sage Essential Oil

2 drops Cleansing Essential Oil Blend

5 drops Outdoor Essential Oil Blend

8 drops Peppermint Essential Oil

4 drops Lemon Essential Oil

2 drops Geranium Essential Oil

2 drops Eucalyptus Essential Oil

3 drops Lavender Essential Oil

2 drops Myrrh Essential Oil

For spray, simply substitute 8 oz. of purified water for 8 oz. of shampoo base.

Spray your dog, bedding and yourself!

Homemade Flea Collar

Mix 4 oz. of distilled water and 10 drops Eucalyptus, 10 drops Repellent Blend and 10 drops Lemongrass essential oils.

Soak a nylon collar in the solution for 20 minutes.

Remove collar and allow it to dry thoroughly before placing it on your pet.

Re-soak the collar every two weeks or more frequently as needed.

Natural Flea Bomb

10 drops Black Pepper Essential Oil

10 drops Oregano Essential Oil

10 drops Wild Orange Essential Oil

10 drops Peppermint Essential Oil

10 drops Cleansing Essential Oil Blend (to be used after "flea bombing" the house)

Add 10 drops each of Black Pepper, Oregano, Wild Orange and Peppermint Essential Oils to a water diffuser or in an empty bottle for a nebulizer diffuser. Open all of the interior doors in your home and place the diffuser in the most central location possible. If there is a heavy infestation in more than one room, you will need to treat each room individually. Turn your diffuser on to maximum output and use a continuous diffusion for 2-3 hours. Leave your home during this time. Upon returning home, open all of the windows in your home. Diffuse Cleansing Blend for another 1-2 hours.

Now, it is time to vacuum everywhere! Move furniture to vacuum behind it and under it. Vacuum the furniture, too. Empty the vacuum when you are finished.

GASTRIC ULCERS

The most common cause of gastric ulceration is the administration of Non-Steroidal Anti-Inflammatory Drugs (NSAID's). This class of medication is used to treat pain and reduce inflammation. Medications in this class include Tylenol, Aspirin, Motrin, and Aleve. If your pet needs to take a non-steroidal medication, your veterinarian will prescribe one tested in dogs and cats and is safe for their use. Do not use medications designated for human consumption on your pets.

Gastric upset, irritation, bleeding and ulcers are more likely to develop when over-the-counter medications are used in high doses or for extended periods of time. Never medicate your pet without consulting your veterinarian. The use of non-steroidal medications (NSAID's) should be closely monitored by your veterinarian with blood work and frequent visits.

If your pet needs a non-steroidal medication, protect your pet's gastrointestinal system from damage with essential oils. The use of anti-inflammatory essential oils may allow you to decrease the amount of medication your pet is taking.

For dogs, apply a combination of Digestive Blend, Myrrh and Lavender, and add Lemon to the drinking water daily, (if there are no cats in the home). This will support and calm the digestive system. For immune support, diffuse Protective Blend. Give your dog a probiotic supplement to further support the gastrointestinal system.

For cats, apply a combination of Digestive Blend, Myrrh and Lavender daily, and add Lavender and/or Digestive Blend to the litter box as described in Litter Box Power. For immune support, diffuse Protective Blend. Give your cat a probiotic supplement to further support the gastrointestinal system.

FOR DOGS

Apply 1-2 drops each Digestive Blend, Lavender and Myrrh once to twice daily.

Add 1 drop of Lemon to two cups drinking water (if there are no cats in the home).

Diffuse Protective Blend for at least 20-30 minutes 2-3 times daily.

Continue probiotic supplements.

FOR CATS

Apply 1 drop each Digestive Blend, Lavender, and Myrrh daily.

Add Lavender and/or Digestive Blend to the litter box as described in Litter Box Power.

Diffuse Protective Blend for at least 20-30 minutes 2-3 times daily.

Continue probiotic supplements.

GROOMING AND BASIC PET CARE

Caring for your pet helps to create and sustain a special bond between you and your pet, which is strengthened by spending time together. Grooming is enjoyable for both you and your pet.

Brush your dog or cat at least three times weekly to maintain a healthy, unknotted coat. Longer haired dogs and cats and those cats prone to hair balls benefit from more frequent brushing, up to daily. We recommend a slicker brush and a wide-toothed comb for most grooming needs, using caution on the face and around the eyes. Speak with your groomer or veterinarian for individual advice.

Dogs that are considered to be non-shedding or hypoallergenic, such as Poodles, Maltese, Shih-Tzu, Bichon Frise, and Terriers, need to be professionally groomed every 3-8 weeks, on average. Hypoallergenic breeds have hair, which continually grows and needs to be trimmed regularly. If your pet is matted or has large knots in their coat, see your groomer or veterinarian for assistance. Do not attempt to cut your dog's hair, since the risk of injury to your pet is high. Leave scissoring or clipping your pet to a professional.

We all appreciate a clean pet, yet bathing too frequently can dry your dog's skin and lead to knots and mats. Cats generally do not accept bathing well, and most cats keep themselves clean without getting a bath their entire lives. It is very important to comb and/or brush your dog after bathing to prevent the hair from forming knots, which may then develop into larger mats. Repeated bathing without proper brushing and combing leads to matting of the coat. Bathing frequently will also remove the monthly liquid flea and tick preventatives, thereby lessening your dog's protection. Bathe your dog with Soothing Skin

Shampoo (See recipe) every 2-4 weeks unless directed by your veterinarian for a medical reason.

Following every bath, clean your dog's ears to prevent infection (See Ear Cleaning and Ear Infections). Routinely, clean your dog's or cat's ears 1-2 times monthly. Increase the frequency of ear cleaning to 2-4 times monthly in warmer, humid weather and after any contact with water such as swimming or exposure to heavy rain.

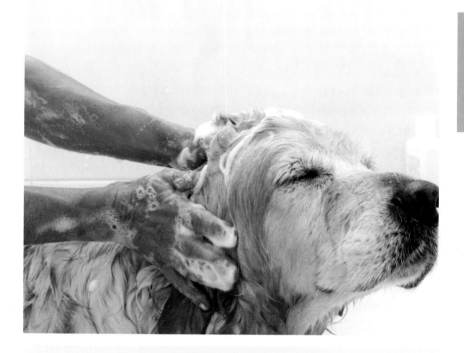

"The most affectionate creature in the world is a wet dog."

- Ambrose Bierce

Nail trimming is generally recommended on a monthly basis. Overgrown nails inhibit proper contact of the paws with the ground or floor and place undue tension on the paws and joints. Walking your dog on concrete helps to wear the nails and extend the time between nail trims. Most dogs and cats do not like having their nails trimmed, so you may need to visit your veterinarian or groomer for periodic nail trims. Each nail contains a blood vessel which grows along with the nail. Be careful not to cut the nails too short and cause bleeding and pain. Cutting the nails too short may easily happen if your pet is struggling, moving, shaking or if the nails have grown very long. Alternatively, you may file your pet's nails weekly with a wide nail file or filing block available at beauty supply stores.

Wet dog smell? When our dogs come in from the rain, they often exude a unique odor. Bathing after every outing is neither practical nor advisable. Dry your pet with a towel, and apply the Pet Powder to remove odors naturally (See recipe). During rainy or snowy months, remove mud and salt by wiping your pet's paws with cleansing cloths, Gentle Cleanser (See recipe) or a damp towel. If you notice an odor from your pet's eyes, ears, paws or any other part of the body, it may indicate an infection. Contact your veterinarian.

If your dog encounters a skunk and is unfortunately for you and your dog sprayed, try to remain calm and use our favorite Skunk Remedy (See recipe) to bathe your pet. It is a combination of vinegar, baking soda and Castile soap or natural dish detergent. Do not wet your dog; immediately apply Skunk Remedy to your dog dry. Be careful to avoid the eyes and ears. Massage the Skunk Remedy for 5 minutes and then rinse well and repeat. After towel drying your dog, spray your dog and diffuse Cleansing Blend as often as needed to remove residual odor. Often, dogs are sprayed in the face and eyes. The skunk's spray may irritate the eyes causing redness, tearing, rubbing and squinting. In this case, see your veterinarian.

FOR DOGS

Bathe every 2-4 weeks or less. Dry thoroughly.

Clean ears 1-2 times monthly (See Ear Cleaning) and 2-4 times monthly in warmer, more humid weather.

Have your groomer or veterinarian trim the nails monthly.

To remove wet dog smell, apply Pet Powder (See recipe) daily as needed.

To remove skunk odor: Do not wet your dog. Bathe with Skunk Remedy (See recipe) massaging for 5 minutes and repeat. Dilute 10 drops Cleansing Blend in 1 oz. purified water, and spray your dog as needed. Diffuse Cleansing Blend to remove odors in your home.

FOR CATS

Brush weekly for short haired cats and 3 times weekly for long haired cats.

Trim nail's monthly if possible or have them trimmed by your veterinarian or groomer.

Bathing is best performed by a professional.

Soothing Skin Shampoo

3 oz. Castile soap (available at many health and bulk food stores)
2 oz. Organic unpasteurized, unfiltered Apple Cider Vinegar
1 oz. Vegetable Glycerin
2 oz. Distilled water
3 drops Lavender Essential Oil
3 drops Roman Chamomile Essential Oil
Optional: add 1 tsp. ground oatmeal

Pet Powder

1 Cup Corn Starch
5 drops Lavender Essential Oil
5 drops Geranium Essential Oil
4 drops Eucalyptus Essential Oil

Mix well, and keep in a small mason jar with several holes in the top. Sprinkle a small amount on your dog and brush him or her. He or she will not only smell great, but repels ticks and other pests.

Skunk Remedy

4 cups Vinegar

¼ cup Baking Soda

2 tsp. Castile soap or natural dish detergent.

Do not wet your dog; immediately apply Skunk Remedy to your dog dry. Be careful to avoid the eyes and ears. Massage the Skunk Remedy for 5 minutes and then rinse well and repeat. After towel drying your dog, spray your dog and diffuse cleansing blend as often as needed to remove residual odor.

HAIRBALLS

Contrary to popular belief, hairballs in cats are not normal. Excessive grooming, anxiety, and poor diet are often the cause. Cats get hairballs from licking their coats and swallowing hair, which accumulates in the stomach and eventually forms a wad. The accompanying discomfort prompts the cat to vomit the hair ball.

Feed your cat a high quality diet with appropriate supplements, and eliminate chemicals in the home. Apply Digestive Blend twice daily to help your cat pass the hairball, and add Digestive Blend to the litter box as described in Litter Box Power. Apply Lavender twice daily to keep your cat calm, and diffuse Calming Blend or Lavender before bed. Brush your cat every 2-3 days to remove excess hair.

FOR CATS

Brush your cat every 2-3 days to remove excess hair.

Apply 1 drop of Digestive Blend twice daily.

Add Digestive Blend to the litter box as described in Litter Box Power.

Diffuse or apply 1 drop of Lavender or Calming Blend before bed.

*In ancient times cats were worshipped
as gods; they have not forgotten this.*

-Terry Pratchett

HEARTWORM DISEASE

Heartworms are very long worms that live in and around the hearts of dogs and cats and obstruct their normal blood flow. Heartworm disease is serious. Dogs and cats with heartworm disease are at risk of death. Heartworms are transmitted by mosquitoes and prevention is critical. (See Fleas, Ticks and Mosquitoes). Although there are reports of essential oil treatments for heartworm disease, we recommend using essential oils as complementary therapy to support a healthy immune system. The incidence of heartworm disease in cats is much lower than in dogs, and there is no traditional medical treatment for it in cats.

Heartworm disease can be found throughout the United States and is more prevalent in areas with a high mosquito population. An annual blood test is recommended for all dogs and cats living in these endemic areas to check for the presence of heartworms. Administer an oral monthly heartworm preventative to your pet as directed by your veterinarian.

Many essential oils have a remarkable ability to both support the immune system and increase one's rate of healing. This is crucial in the prevention of heartworm disease and if your pet contracts this disease. Some of these same essential oils are also powerful antiseptics. One way these oils fight infection is to stimulate the production of white blood cells, which are part of the body's immune defense. Still other essential oils encourage new cell growth to promote faster healing. Lemon and rosemary essential oils found in the Protective Blend stimulate the lymphatic system to circulate the blood around the body and remove waste and infection.

For dogs, support your pet with topical Helichrysum and Oregano (diluted). Add Protective Blend or Lemon to drinking water (if there are no cats in the home). Diffuse Protective Blend daily.

For cats, support your pet with topical Helichrysum and Myrrh. Diffuse Protective Blend daily.

FOR DOGS

Apply 1-2 drops of Helichrysum twice daily.

Dilute 1 drop of Oregano in 4 Tbsp. of carrier oil and apply 1-2 drops twice daily.

Add 1 drop of Protective Blend to 2 cups drinking water. (if there are no cats in the home).

Diffuse Protective Blend at least 20-30 minutes 2-3 times daily.

FOR CATS

Apply 1 drop each Helichrysum and Myrrh twice daily.

Diffuse Protective Blend at least 20-30 minutes 2-3 daily.

Note: Although there are reports of essential oils eliminating heartworms in dogs, we recommend traditional therapies and medications for treatment of this serious illness. In fact, the safest practice is strict control of mosquitoes (See Fleas, Ticks and Mosquitoes) and the administration of a monthly preventative tablet or chewable.

HEAT STROKE (HYPERTHERMIA)

Pets overheat very easily. For this reason, never leave your pet in a car on a hot or warm day. Pets can suffer heat stroke even if the car windows are open. When spending time outside in the warmer weather, bring water, seek breaks in the shade and watch your pet carefully. Signs of heat stroke include panting, excessive salivation, pale or red gums, difficulty breathing, disorientation, lack of coordination, passing out or seizures.

A pet's normal body temperature is between 100-103 degrees Fahrenheit. The most accurate method of taking a pet's temperature is rectally.

Call your veterinarian. Heat stroke is an emergency which requires monitoring in the hospital and intravenous fluid therapy. Many pets suffering from hyperthermia are in shock, so do not waste time offering your pet water. They generally will not drink water in this condition.

When a pet's body temperature becomes too high, brain damage or even death may ensue. Quickly reduce your pet's body temperature. For dogs, apply Peppermint or Soothing Blend to the inside of the ear flaps, paws, abdomen and inner thighs. Give dogs 1-2 drops of Peppermint by mouth. For cats, apply Soothing Blend (diluted) and substitute Lavender for Peppermint. For both dogs and cats, apply Frankincense, Helichrysum and Lavender topically 4-6 times daily.

Wintergreen, found in a soothing blend

FOR DOGS

 Seek veterinary care immediately.

Immediately apply 1-2 drops Soothing Blend or Peppermint to the ear flaps, paws, abdomen and inner thighs hourly.

Apply 1 drop each Frankincense, Helichrysum, and Lavender hourly.

Give 1-2 drops Peppermint orally hourly.

FOR CATS

 Seek veterinary care immediately.

Immediately, dilute 1 drop Soothing Blend in 4 Tbsp. of carrier oil. Combine 1 drop of diluted Soothing Blend with 1 drop of Lavender and apply to the ear flaps, paws, abdomen and inner thighs every 2 hours. Avoid Peppermint in cats.

Apply 1 drop Frankincense, Helichrysum, and Lavender every 2 hours.

HYPOGLYCEMIA (LOW BLOOD SUGAR)

Young dogs and cats, small puppies and kittens are at the highest risk for hypoglycemia. Most commonly, hypoglycemic puppies and kittens are not eating well or are ill. Young dogs of certain breeds born with a congenital liver shunt may demonstrate signs of hypoglycemia. Other metabolic conditions can decrease blood sugar in pets of all ages.

Another common cause of hypoglycemia is xylitol toxicity. Xylitol is a sweetener found in many household products such as gum, vitamins, medications, antacids and toothpaste.

In diabetic pets, an overdose of insulin or insulin given without a meal may result in low blood sugar.

Signs of hypoglycemia include seizures, weakness, collapse, lethargy, disorientation, incoordination and excessive thirst and hunger.

Be careful giving young pets sugar supplements with the intention of maintaining blood sugar. These products, which may be falsely marketed as vitamin supplements, often contain high fructose corn syrup. They are taken into the body quickly and result in an immediate rise in blood sugar followed by a rapid decline in blood sugar.

Owners are then likely to administer the sugary supplement again, entering a cycle of high and low fluctuations in blood sugar. Rather than sugar supplements, feed a high quality diet several times daily.

If you suspect hypoglycemia, offer your pet food and call your veterinarian. If your pet is too listless to eat, you may offer a liquid sugar product such as Karo syrup via syringe. Apply Frankincense and Peppermint for dogs and Frankincense and Lavender for cats (do not use peppermint oil in cats). See your veterinarian right away.

FOR DOGS

 Seek veterinary care immediately.

Immediately apply 1-2 drops Soothing Blend or Peppermint to the ear flaps, paws, abdomen and inner thighs hourly.

Apply 1 drop each Frankincense, Helichrysum, and Lavender hourly.

Give 1-2 drops Peppermint orally hourly.

FOR CATS

 Seek veterinary care immediately.

Immediately apply diluted 1 drop Soothing Blend in 4 Tbsp. of carrier oil to the ear flaps, paws, abdomen and inner thighs every 2 hours. Avoid Peppermint in cats.

Apply 1 drop each Frankincense, Helichrysum, and Lavender every 2 hours.

HYPOTHYROIDISM (UNDER-ACTIVE THYROID)

Hypothyroidism is a slowed metabolism due to an underproduction of thyroid hormone. This condition generally affects middle aged dogs, and certain breeds are more likely to develop an under active thyroid. Hypothyroidism is very rare in cats. Most of the cases of hypothyroidism are immune-mediated or idiopathic, meaning that no known cause has been identified. In some cases, it is suspected that hypothyroidism may be associated with environmental toxins.

Since thyroid hormone is involved in so many body systems, the signs of hypothyroidism can vary. Most dogs that are affected are lethargic, gain weight and have dry, flaky skin (See Dry Skin). Additional signs include chronic skin and ear infections (See Ear Infections), increased thirst, attraction to heat, seizures (See Seizures) and aggressive and irritable behavior. See your veterinarian for a physical exam and appropriate diagnostic testing. Traditionally, hypothyroidism is treated by administering synthetic thyroid hormone.

Lemongrass

Essential oils may be used in hypothyroidism to complement traditional therapy and may reduce the amount of medication needed.

Apply Lemongrass, Frankincense and Myrrh daily. Diffuse Lemongrass, Frankincense and Myrrh, alternating oils. Add Protective Blend or Lemon to drinking water to support the immune system, (if there are no cats in the home).

Other essential oils may be used to address your dog's specific symptoms. Apply or diffuse Joyful Blend, citrus oils and Peppermint to reduce lethargy and depression. Apply or diffuse Grounding Blend to lessen anxiety and irritability.
Since an under-active thyroid is a chronic condition, which will need to be managed for the rest of your pet's life, consistency of the application of essential oils is very important.

FOR DOGS

Combine 5 drops Lemongrass, 2 drops Frankincense, and 5 drops Myrrh. Dilute this mixture in 2 Tbsp. of carrier oil, and apply 1-2 drops twice daily.

Add 1 drop of Protective Blend or Lemon to 2 cups drinking water (if there are no cats in the home).

Diffuse Lemongrass, Frankincense and Myrrh for 30-60 minutes twice daily, alternating oils.

Clean and launder with natural cleaners. Avoid plastic food bowls and toys.

LIPOMAS OR FATTY TUMORS

Lipomas are very common in dogs of all ages and breeds. In some cases, these benign tumors greatly increase in size, becoming not only unsightly, but may also interfere with the pet's ability to walk, run or play comfortably. Any lump, bump or growth should be evaluated by your veterinarian.

Essential oils can help to reduce the size of any lump, thereby reducing your pet's discomfort and increasing mobility. Applying essential oils when a lump is first noticed, may prevent the lump from increasing in size and interfering with your pet's healthy activity.

Massage the lipoma with Lime or Grapefruit and Frankincense, which have been found to be anti-tumoral. Consistent application will offer the best outcome. Results may take several months.

FOR DOGS

See your veterinarian for a diagnosis.

Massage the lipoma with 1-2 drops Lime or Grapefruit and 1-2 drops Frankincense 2-4 times daily. Consistent application will offer the best outcome. Results may take several months.

Grapefruit

"Cats are the natural companions of intellectuals. They are silent watchers of dreams, inspiration and patient research."

- Dr. Fernand Mery

LITTER BOX POWER

Many cats and kittens are difficult to medicate, especially once they are aware of their owners' intent, no matter how benevolent it may be. One technique to influence our cats' behavior or to treat illness is to add an essential oil to the litter box. To do this, add 1-2 drops of the chosen essential oil to 1 cup of baking soda. Allow the mixture to rest overnight in a glass jar. Add 1 tablespoon of the mixture of essential oil and baking soda recipe to the litter box. The aromatic benefits of the essential oils will be released into the air as your cat steps in the box and paws at the litter.

We recommend adding 1 Tbsp. and monitoring your cat for a day. Provide a second litter box which does not contain essential oils to allow the cats time to acclimate to the new litter box. Once you are sure that your cat is not experiencing any adverse effects, you may remove the untreated litter box or add 1 tablespoon of the essential oil baking soda mixture to all litter boxes in the home.

Essential oils added to the litter box may help alleviate a number of conditions. For example, add Digestive Blend for cats who suffer from inflammatory bowel disease, vomiting, diarrhea or stress colitis. A nervous or anxious cat may benefit from Lavender added to the litter box, especially in a busy home, filled with visitors or when you go away on vacation. Choose Cleansing Blend, Lemongrass, or Wild Orange to control odors naturally.

Pine, found in a cleansing blend

Litter Box Power

Add 1-2 drops of the chosen essential oil (ex. Digestive Blend, Lavender, Cleansing Blend, Lemongrass, or Wild Orange) to 1 cup of baking soda.

Allow the mixture to rest overnight in a glass jar.

Add 1 Tbsp. of the mixture of essential oil and baking soda recipe to the litter box daily.

LUMPS AND BUMPS

As you pet, bathe or brush your pet have you felt any lumps or bumps on their body? Unsightly growths are very common in pets, especially as they age. Many lumps, bumps, skin tags and cysts develop randomly, yet some, such as papillomas and warts are often caused by viruses. Cysts are often the result of blocked hair follicles. The group of growths discussed in this section is benign and is limited to the skin (See Lipomas, Cancer). Essential oils have been shown to be very effective in treating skin growths, particularly warts.

See your veterinarian to evaluate any change in your pet's skin.

For warts, apply Oregano (diluted in dogs) and Melaleuca (diluted in cats) and Myrrh to the area of concern daily. The wart or growth may appear worse initially, then fall off. Subsequently, the skin will heal over the next several days. For immune support, diffuse Protective Blend daily. For other benign growths, essential oils may prevent the growth from increasing in size and may even reduce its size. Apply Frankincense and Lavender on all lumps, bumps and growths daily. To promote healing and immune support, always feed your pet a high quality diet supplement with Omega-3 and probiotics.

FOR DOGS

Warts: Dilute 1 drop Oregano in 4 Tbsp. carrier oil. Apply 1 drop each of diluted Oregano and Melaleuca 2-3 times daily.

Diffuse Protective Blend 20-30 minutes 2-3 times daily.

Feed your pet a high quality diet supplement with Omega-3 and probiotics.

FOR CATS

Warts: Dilute 1 drop Melaleuca in 4 Tbsp. carrier oil. Apply 1 drop each of diluted Melaleuca and Myrrh 2-3 times daily.

Diffuse Protective Blend 20-30 minutes 2-3 times daily.

Feed your pet a high quality diet supplement with Omega-3 and probiotics.

FOR DOGS & CATS

Lumps, Bumps and Growths : Apply 1-2 drops each of Frankincense and Lavender 2-3 times daily.

Diffuse Protective Blend 20-30 minutes 2-3 times daily.

Feed your pet a high quality diet supplement with Omega-3 and probiotics.

MASTITIS

Mastitis is an inflammation and/or infection of the mammary glands, which may develop during nursing puppies or kittens. The mammary glands become red, inflamed, hard and painful. Milk production may decrease and the newborns may fail to grow well.

If the mother is feverish, not eating well or refusing to nurse, see your veterinarian. Monitor the puppies' or kittens' growth by weighing them on a gram scale every 2-3 days. If they are not gaining weight, contact your veterinarian.

Clean the mother's mammary glands with a natural cleanser (See Gentle Cleanser) 1-2 times daily. Pat dry, and apply an ointment such as Healing Salve (See recipe) 2-4 times daily. Try to apply the salve at times of the day when the puppies or kittens are less likely to be nursing, so that the salve may be absorbed well.

For dogs, apply Oregano (diluted) and Myrrh 2-4 times daily and add Protective Blend to drinking water (if there are not cats in the home). For puppies, apply Frankincense well absorbed to your hands, and pet your puppy and diffuse Protective Blend to support your new born puppy's immune system. To alleviate any stress in the household, diffuse or apply Lavender or Calming Blend to yourself and the mother twice daily.

For cats, apply Oregano (diluted) and Myrrh twice daily. For kittens, apply Frankincense, well absorbed to your hands, and pet your kitten. Diffuse Protective Blend to support your new born kitten's immune system. To alleviate any stress in the household, diffuse or apply Lavender or Calming Blend to yourself and the mother twice daily.

FOR DOGS

Clean the mother's mammary glands 1-2 times daily with Gentle Cleanser (See recipe).

Apply Healing Salve (See recipe) to the mammary glands 2-4 times daily.

Dilute 2 drops of Oregano in 2-4 Tbsp. of carrier oil apply 1 drop twice daily.

Add 1 drop of Protective Blend to the drinking water (if there are no cats in the home).

Diffuse Protective Blend, Calming Blend or Lavender for 20-30 minutes 2-3 times daily.

Apply 1 drop of Frankincense, well absorbed into your hands, to the puppies daily.

FOR CATS

Clean the mother's mammary glands 1-2 times daily with Gentle Cleanser (See recipe).

Apply Healing Salve (See recipe) to the mammary glands 2-4 times daily.

Dilute 1 drop of Oregano in 2-4 Tbsp. of carrier oil apply 1 drop twice daily.

Diffuse Protective Blend, Calming Blend or Lavender for 20-30 minutes 2-3 times daily.

Apply 1 drop of Frankincense, well absorbed into your hands, to the kittens daily.

Gentle Cleanser

4 ounces Castile soap or unscented natural foaming soap
2 drops Roman Chamomile Essential Oil
2 drops Lavender Essential Oil

Healing Salve

8 ounces Cold-Pressed Organic Coconut Oil
1 ounce Beeswax
2 drops Vitamin E (optional)
10 drops Lavender Essential Oil
5 drops Myrrh Essential Oil
3 drops Helichrysum Essential Oil
Glass Jars or Tin Containers

Place the coconut oil and beeswax over a double –boiler, and gently warm over low heat until the beeswax melts. Remove from heat and add the essential oils and Vitamin E oil, (if using). Quickly pour the mixture into glass jars or tins, and allow to cool completely. Store salve in a cool location where it will not re-melt and re-solidify. When stored correctly, salve will last for 1-3 years. Yields 8 oz.

NEW PET PARENTS / INTRODUCING A NEW PET

Congratulations on your new pet! Introducing a new pet into your home with or without other pets is a big change for both you and your pet. Be patient. Many pets take weeks to months to fully acclimate.

Practice close supervision. Confining a new puppy or dog to 1-2 rooms, usually the kitchen, will allow you to watch him or her more carefully. As he or she becomes comfortable, is housebroken and proves to be trustworthy, the allotted space may be increased. When you are not home or not able to provide supervision, we suggest that your new puppy or dog be confined to a crate.

Keep a new kitten or cat in one room with food, water, and a litter box. Allow other cats to sniff and paw at him or her under the door. After 1-2 weeks and a thorough veterinary exam, your new addition may explore a greater area of the home while you are present. Be sure the litter box is not very far away. The general rule is to provide 1 litter box per cat plus one extra in various locations throughout your home. Scoop the litter boxes daily and fully clean them weekly.

Allow contact or play between pets only under supervision until you feel comfortable that they are amicable. To ease this transition, apply Calming Blend and Grounding Blend daily as needed. Diffuse Calming Blend or Grounding Blend especially when you expect moments of agitation, stress, or nervousness. Soft music and dim lighting also promote restfulness and calming. For pets that are fearful or are taking a long time to adjust to their new home, apply Frankincense twice daily.

"I had been told that the training procedure with cats was difficult. It's not. Mine had me trained in two days."

–Bill Dana

FOR DOGS & CATS

Apply 1-2 drops Calming Blend and Grounding Blend 2-4 times daily.

For difficult transitions, apply 1-2 drops Frankincense twice daily.

Diffuse Calming Blend and/or Grounding Blend as needed.

NUTRITION-THE FOUNDATION OF HEALTH

Nutrition is the foundation of good health for your pet. A healthy, balanced diet optimizes your pet's immune system, their organ function, and helps them to live long and healthy lives. Good health is built upon a base of excellent nutrition.

Essential oils help deliver nutrients to all the cells of the body. Applying essential oils to your pet or adding essential oils to your dog's drinking water (if there are no cats in the home) is an easy and effective way to increase the availability and absorption of nutrition. For dogs, add citrus oils to the drinking water (if there are no cats in the home) to support the immune system and improve digestion. For cats, apply Lavender and Myrrh daily to support the immune system and the digestive system. For dogs and cats, apply Frankincense daily to support overall wellbeing.

Two supplements, a probiotic and Omega 3 (fish oil), are especially important, even if your pet eats a high quality diet. A probiotic and a fish oil supplement are not only valuable for excellent health, but they also provide particularly helpful benefits for animals affected by seasonal and other allergies. Since most of the immune system resides in the gut, a probiotic directly supports a healthy immune system as well as fortifying the digestive system. Fish oil reduces inflammation in the body, reducing itchy skin, redness and irritation.

Feed your pet a high quality diet. Be sure that the first ingredient is a protein such as beef, lamb, fish, chicken or soy and that all of the ingredients are recognizable, not a list of unpronounceable chemicals. Beyond these basics, you may look for phrases such as "human grade, "no byproducts" and "organic" to indicate the high degree of quality of the pet food. High quality pet foods are sold at stores dedicated to pets or by your veterinarian.

A recent surge of grain-free diets have arrived on the market. Grain-free formulas are ideal for pets with known food allergies, particularly allergies to grains. Some pets with digestive issues, skin sensitivities, or seasonal allergies may also benefit from a grain-free diet. For most other pets, grain-free formulas are optional. Some pets suffer from protein allergies and may require a prescription diet. (See Allergies.)

An added benefit of a high quality pet food is often evident in the yard or litter box. A highly digestible diet (one without fillers) produces less fecal matter. Although a high quality diet may cost more initially, most pets eat less since every bite is full of good, digestible nutrition. Interestingly, most high quality pet foods are not advertised on television. Choose a pet food that your pet likes, is affordable and is also convenient for you to find in your local pet store or online.

FOR DOGS

Add 1 drop of citrus oils to 2 cups drinking water (if there are no cats in the home).

Apply 1 drop Frankincense daily.

FOR CATS

Apply 1 drop Frankincense daily.

Apply 1 drop each of Myrrh and Lavender daily.

OBSESSIVE-COMPULSIVE DISORDER (OCD)

Obsessive-Compulsive Disorder (OCD) can develop for a number of reasons, most commonly moving to a new home, welcoming a new baby, or changes in family work schedules. Often, the source of stress or anxiety cannot be easily identified. Both dogs and cats can suffer from OCD in different ways (See Anxiety).

Cats with OCD tend to over groom to the point of removing their hair, termed psychogenic alopecia. Additionally, they may refuse to use the litter box and hide.

Some dogs with this condition tend to lick or bite at their front legs, paws or flanks (the area between the last rib and the rear leg), causing severe wounds and permanent damage to the skin. The skin may be so badly damaged that it scars and may never grow hair back (See Cuts, & Scrapes). Other dogs circle repeatedly, chase their tails, chew furniture or other household items (See Chewing), or lick the sofa or bedspread for extended periods of time. Causes of such anxiety may be breed-associated or hereditary, the result of prior maltreatment or abuse, neglect, boredom or nervousness.

See your veterinarian for a physical exam and appropriate diagnostic testing. OCD may be so severe that some pets need traditional medication to prevent them from harming or endangering themselves. Talk to your veterinarian or consult a behaviorist for assistance.

Essential oils offer complementary therapy and may reduce the amount of medication needed and may even eliminate the need for medication.

"In order to keep a true perspective of one's importance, everyone should have a dog that will worship him and a cat that will ignore him."

- Derek Bruce

Help calm your pet(s) with Calming Blend and Grounding Blend. Diffuse Calming Blend and Grounding Blend, alternating essential oils. You may find that your pet responds best to a particular oil or to a specific application method, such as using a spray, diffuser, or topical application. For example, a spray vs. direct topical application vs. diffusing. Your pet may also be more anxious during different times of the day or night, depending on the activity in the household and may benefit from essential oils during these particular times.

For severe cases of OCD in dogs, try applying Frankincense, Cedarwood, and Bergamot daily. These may be used in addition to the Calming Blend and Grounding Blend.

For cats, apply Calming Blend or Lavender daily. Add Calming Blend or Grounding Blend to the litter box as described in Litter Box Power.

Lastly, pets are very sensitive to our moods and stress levels. We lead very busy lives and rush around trying to handle our jobs, home, and family life. Use any of the essential oils listed above to help you remain balanced. The calmer you are, the calmer your pets will be.

FOR DOGS

Apply 1-2 drops Calming Blend and Grounding Blend twice daily.

Diffuse Calming Blend and Grounding Blend for at least 20-30 minutes 2-3 times daily.

For severe cases of OCD, apply 1-2 drops Calming Blend and Grounding Blend twice daily.

Apply 1 drop each of Frankincense, Cedarwood, and Bergamot twice daily.

Diffuse Calming Blend and Grounding Blend at least 20-30 minutes 2-3 times daily.

FOR CATS

Apply 1 drop Calming Blend or Lavender and either Myrrh or Frankincense twice daily.

Add Calming Blend or Grounding Blend to the litter box as described in Litter Box Power.

Diffuse Calming Blend and Grounding Blend at least 20-30 minutes 2-3 times daily.

ORGAN SUPPORT

Heart, Liver and Kidney conditions should be closely monitored by your veterinarian.

Heart disease most often develops as pets age, in some cases it may be the result of a congenital defect or Heartworm Disease (See Heartworm). As heart disease progresses, the heart enlarges, and puts stress on the respiratory system (See Respiratory Conditions). Most often this will appear as a chronic cough.

Liver disease can develop in pets as they age. In some cases, it may be congenital, the result of an infection or toxins. Signs of liver disease are vomiting, diarrhea, lethargy, and anorexia. In more severe cases, your pet may be jaundiced, a yellowish discoloration to skin, eyes, ears and gums.

Kidney disease is often associated with old age and can also result from infections, toxins, and other metabolic diseases. Some signs are increased thirst and urinations, and weight loss.

Essential oils may offer organ support and reduce the amount of medications your pet needs. Topical Detoxification Blend supports optimum function by cleansing out toxins from liver, kidneys and bladder, helping these organs to work more efficiently. All pets benefit from good hydration, sleep, good nutrition and a probiotic supplement to support and strengthen their immune system.

For dogs with Heart Disease (Cardiac Disease), apply Helichrysum and Ylang Ylang daily. To support the respiratory system and easeful breathing, apply and diffuse Respiratory Blend or Eucalyptus. To improve blood circulation, apply Massage Blend or Cypress and Lavender daily.

For cats with Heart Disease (Cardiac Disease), apply Helichrysum and Ylang Ylang daily and add Helichrysum to the litter box as described in Litter Box Power. To support the respiratory system and easeful breathing, apply and diffuse Respiratory Blend or Eucalyptus. To improve blood circulation, apply Massage Blend (diluted) or Cypress and Lavender daily.

"My little dog -- a heartbeat at my feet."

-Edith Wharton

For dogs with Kidney Disease (Renal Disease and Hypertension), apply Juniper Berry and Helichrysum daily to aid kidney function. Apply Grapefruit or Invigorating Blend daily and add Grapefruit to drinking water (if there are no cats in the home) to assist the kidneys in eliminating toxins. Apply Ylang Ylang to improve hypertension/decrease blood pressure.

For cats with Kidney Disease (Renal Disease and Hypertension), apply Juniper Berry and Helichrysum daily to aid kidney function and add Ylang Ylang to the litter box as described in Litter Box Power to improve hypertension/decrease blood pressure.

For dogs with Liver Disease (Hepatic Disease), apply Helichrysum and Myrrh and add Grapefruit or Lemon essential oils to drinking water(if there are no cats in the home).

For cats with Liver Disease (Hepatic Disease), apply Helichrysum and Myrrh daily, and add Myrrh to the litter box as described in Litter Box Power.

FOR DOGS

Heart Disease: Apply 1-2 drops Helichrysum and Ylang Ylang 1-2 times daily.

Apply 1-2 drops Respiratory Blend or Eucalyptus 1-2 times daily.

Apply 1-2 drops Massage Blend or Cypress and Lavender 1-2 times daily.

Diffuse Respiratory Blend or Eucalyptus for at least 20-30 minutes 2-3 times daily.

FOR CATS

Heart Disease: Apply 1 drop each Helichrysum and Ylang Ylang to the palms of your hand, let most of the oil absorb and pet your cat daily.

Dilute 1 drop Massage Blend in 4 Tbsp. of carrier oil. Apply 1 drop diluted Massage Blend or Cypress and Lavender to the palms of your hand, let most of the oil absorb and pet your cat daily.

Apply 1 drop each Respiratory Blend or Eucalyptus to the palms of your hand, let most of the oil absorb and pet your cat daily.

Diffuse Respiratory Blend or Eucalyptus for at least 20 -30 minutes 2-3 times daily.

Add Helichrysum to the litter box as described in Litter Box Power.

FOR DOGS

Kidney Disease: Apply 2 drops each of Juniper and Helichrysum 1-2 times daily.

Apply 2 drops Grapefruit or Invigorating Blend 1-2 times daily.

Apply 2 drops Ylang Ylang 1-2 times daily.

Add 1 drop Grapefruit to 2 cups drinking water (if there are no cats in the home).

FOR CATS

Kidney Disease: Apply 1 drop each of Juniper and Helichrysum 1-2 times daily.

Add Ylang Ylang to the litter box as described in Litter Box Power.

FOR DOGS

Liver Disease: Apply 2 drops each Helichrysum and Myrrh daily.

Add 1 drop Grapefruit or Lemon essential oils to 2 cups drinking water (if there are no cats in the home).

FOR CATS

Liver Disease: Apply 1 drop each Helichrysum and Myrrh 1-2 times daily.

Add Myrrh to the litter box as described in Litter Box Power.

PAIN

Pain is so powerful that it can actually inhibit healing and suppresses the immune system. Signs of pain include vocalization, restlessness or agitation, abnormal posture, difficulty moving around, trembling, reduced appetite, stupor or biting. You may also notice a faster than normal heartbeat and rapid breathing.

For dogs, apply Soothing Blend, Helichrysum, Lavender, Marjoram, Myrrh or Peppermint (avoid peppermint in cats). Add Helichrysum and Myrrh to the drinking water (if there are no cats in the home). For cats, apply Soothing Blend (diluted), Helichrysum, Lavender, Marjoram, or Myrrh. Add Lavender and Myrrh to the litter box as described in Litter Box Power.

"They motivate us to play, be affectionate, seek adventure, and be loyal."

‐Tom Hayden

Lavender

FOR DOGS

Apply 1-2 drops of Soothing Blend, Marjoram, and any ONE of the following oils: Helichrysum, Myrrh or Lavender 2-4 times daily.

Add 1 drop each of Helichrysum and Myrrh in 2 cups of drinking water (if there are no cats in the home).

FOR CATS

Dilute 1 drop of Soothing Blend in 4 Tbsp. of carrier oil. Combine 1 drop of diluted Soothing Blend with 1 drop of Myrrh and ONE of the following oils: Helichrysum, or Lavender 1-2 times daily.

Add Lavender and Myrrh to the litter box as described in Litter Box Power.

PANCREATITIS

Pancreatitis is a very painful condition in which the pancreas becomes inflamed. Pets with pancreatitis are ill. Signs include vomiting (more common in dogs), anorexia, lethargy, depression and weight loss (especially in cats). The abdomen becomes painful, pets often have difficulty getting into a comfortable position, are reluctant to lie down, and guard their abdomens. Dogs may display "praying position" where their elbows are resting on the floor and their tail area is held up in the air. This position eases abdominal pressure and pain.

Pancreatitis is diagnosed by a physical, blood tests, x-rays and ultrasound. Pancreatitis is serious and requires hospitalization, IV fluids and close medical attention. Call your veterinarian if your pet is showing any of the above signs.

Causes of pancreatitis include overeating, eating foods high in fat, abrupt changes in diet, viruses, and unknown causes. Certain breeds of dogs are predisposed to developing pancreatitis.

Essential oils can be used to relieve abdominal discomfort, decrease inflammation, and offer your pet symptom relief. Apply Digestive Blend, Frankincense, Lavender, and Soothing Blend daily. Add Lemon to drinking water (if there are no cats in the home). Diffuse Protective Blend to support your pet's immune system and Calming Blend or Lavender to keep you and your pet calm.

FOR DOGS

Apply 1-2 drops each Digestive Blend and Soothing Blend 2-4 times daily.

Apply 1 drop Frankincense 1-2 times daily.

Add 1 drop Lemon to 2 cups drinking water (if there are no cats in the home).

Diffuse Protective Blend for 20-30 minutes 2-3 times daily.

Diffuse Calming Blend or Lavender for 20-30 minutes 2-3 times daily.

FOR CATS

Apply 1 drop Digestive Blend 2 times daily.

Dilute 1 drop Soothing Blend in 4 Tbsp. of carrier oil and apply 2 times daily.

Apply 1 drop Frankincense 1-2 times daily.

Diffuse Protective Blend for 20-30 minutes 2-3 times daily.

Diffuse Calming Blend or Lavender for 20-30 minutes 2-3 times daily.

POISONING

Pets are often curious. Be sure to keep chemicals, medications and vitamin supplements away from pets (See Burns for a complete list of safety recommendations and for information on chemical burns).

The two most common toxicities are ingestion of rat poison and antifreeze. Ingestion of antifreeze (ethylene glycol) has the highest fatality rate of all pet poisonings. These products, and all toxic substances, should not be kept anywhere in your home, basement or garage.

 Poisonings are emergencies. Contact Animal Poison Control* and your veterinarian immediately.

*Animal Poison Control Hotline : 1-800-548-2423

"The gift which I am sending you is called a dog and is in fact the most precious and valuable possesion of mankind."

- Theodorus Gaza

PREGNANCY, LABOR AND DELIVERY

Is your pet expecting? How exciting! Keeping your pet healthy during this time is critical so your pet will have an easy pregnancy and delivery and will give birth to healthy new kittens and puppies.

Good nutrition will keep your pets healthy and support them during pregnancy. Feed your pet a high quality puppy or kitten diet and speak to your veterinarian about additional supplementation.

"Happiness is a warm puppy."

- Charles M Schulz

Essential oils are beneficial for supporting your pet's immune system during pregnancy. Births are exciting and stressful for all. Essential oils will help to keep you and your pet calm during pregnancy. Try to prepare a quiet, comfortable area for the mother. Ease the stress of an impending birth by creating a supportive and healthy environment.

Apply Frankincense and Myrrh to the mother during pregnancy and delivery to prevent infection and to support the immune system. Apply Lavender or Calming Blend throughout the pregnancy, labor and delivery to keep you and the expectant mother calm. Diffuse Frankincense, Roman Chamomile, Calming Blend or Lavender throughout the birthing process to create a calm and healthy atmosphere.

Once the kittens or puppies are born, welcome them into the world by anointing them on the crown of the head with Frankincense. Apply Frankincense and Myrrh to the cut umbilical cords.

To foster healthy milk production, lactation, or to increase milk production, apply Fennel at the onset of labor and during nursing. For dogs, add Fennel to the drinking water (if there are no cats in the home).

FOR DOGS & CATS

Pregnancy: Apply 1-2 drops of Frankincense and Myrrh topically to the mother twice daily.

Apply 1-2 drops of Lavender or Calming Blend twice daily.

Diffuse Frankincense, Roman Chamomile, Calming Blend or Lavender for 20-30 minutes 2-3 times daily.

Feed a high quality puppy or kitten food throughout the pregnancy.

Labor and Delivery: Apply 1-2 drops of Frankincense and Myrrh topically every 2 hours.

Apply 1-2 drops of Lavender or Calming Blend every 2 hours.

Diffuse Frankincense, Roman Chamomile, Calming Blend or Lavender for 20-30 minutes 2-3 times daily.

After Birth: Apply 1-2 drops of Frankincense to the crown of the head of the newborn.

Apply 1 drop each Frankincense and Myrrh to the newborns' cut umbilical cords.

Apply 1-2 drops of Frankincense and Myrrh topically to the mother twice daily.

Apply 1-2 drops of Lavender or Calming Blend twice daily to the mother.

Diffuse Frankincense, Roman Chamomile, Calming Blend or Lavender for 20-30 minutes 2-3 times daily.

FOR DOGS

Lactation: Apply 1-2 drops Fennel 2-4 times daily.
Add 1 drop Fennel to 2 cups drinking water (if there are no cats in the home).

Feed a high quality puppy food throughout lactation.

FOR CATS

Lactation: Apply 1 drop Fennel 2-4 times daily.

Feed a high quality kitten food throughout lactation.

PROSTATIC DISEASE

Prostatic disease typically affects older male intact (not neutered) dogs, at an average age of 8-9 years. Cats rarely develop prostatic disease. Enlargement of the prostate is directly influenced by testosterone, so neutered males are not affected.

The prostate gland is located at the base of the bladder. If the prostate gland becomes enlarged, it constricts the flow of urine through the urethra. The prostate may also become infected, abscessed or develop cysts.

Signs of prostatic disease include difficulty urinating, discolored or bloody urine, and discharge from the penis. Additional signs are lethargy, loss of appetite, abdominal pain, fever, and vomiting.

See your veterinarian if you notice any of the above signs in your dog. Prostatic disease is diagnosed with a physical exam, blood tests, x-rays and ultrasound. Prostatic disease is treated with antibiotics and by neutering your pet.

Essential oils can assist your dog by reducing inflammation and fighting bacteria. To reduce inflammation, apply Frankincense, Helichrysum, and Lavender daily. For prostatic infections, secondary urinary tract infections and prostatic abscesses, apply Oregano (diluted) daily.

Oregano

FOR DOGS

Apply 1-2 drops each Frankincense, Helichrysum and Lavender twice daily.

For prostatic infections, secondary urinary tract infections and prostatic abscesses, dilute 1 drop Oregano in 2-4 Tbsp. of carrier oil, apply twice daily.

Continue to feed your pet a healthy diet and supplement Omega-3 and probiotics.

PYOMETRA (UTERINE INFECTION)

Pyometra develops in intact (not spayed) female dogs and cats when the uterus becomes infected and fills with pus. Signs of a pyometra include lethargy, decreased appetite, drinking excessively, fever and vaginal discharge. Pyometra usually occurs 2 months after a female dog's heat cycle (estrus). Female cats can develop a pyometra at any time in their reproductive cycles.

If you notice any of these signs, call your veterinarian. A pyometra is an emergency and can be fatal.

Your veterinarian will diagnose a pyometra with a physical exam, blood tests, x-rays and ultrasound. The uterus, quickly filling with pus, is at risk of rupture and must be removed right away. The treatment for a pyometra is to spay your dog or cat immediately. Pets with pyometra often remain in the veterinary hospital and are treated with antibiotics, fluid therapy, and pain relief.

Essential oils can support your pet's immune system, promote healing and fight bacteria. For dogs, apply a combination of Frankincense, Helichrysum and Geranium daily to reduce inflammation. Use a mixture of Oregano (diluted), Melaleuca, and Lavender daily to limit infection and promote healing. Support the immune system by adding Lemon to drinking water (if there are no cats in the home) and diffusing Protective Blend. Apply Soothing Blend as needed for pain.

For cats, apply a combination of Frankincense, Myrrh and Geranium daily. Fight infection and promote healing by applying Melaleuca (diluted) and Lavender daily. Daily use of Soothing Blend may be used to reduce pain, and diffuse Protective Blend to support the immune system.

FOR DOGS

Apply 1-2 drops Frankincense, Helichrysum and Geranium 2-3 times daily.

Dilute 1 drop of Oregano in 2-4 Tbsp. carrier oil. Apply 1-2 drops diluted Oregano or Melaleuca and Lavender 2-3 times daily.

Apply 1-2 drops Soothing Blend 2-4 times daily as needed for pain.

Add 1 drop of Lemon to 2 cups of drinking water (if there are no cats in the home).

Diffuse Protective Blend for at least 20-30 minutes 2-3 times daily.

Feed your pet a high quality diet and continue supplementing with Omega-3 and probiotics.

FOR CATS

Apply 1 drop each Frankincense, Myrrh and Geranium 1-2 times daily.

Dilute Melaleuca 1 drop in 4 Tbsp. of carrier oils. Apply 1 drop each of diluted Melaleuca and Lavender 1-2 times daily.

Dilute 1 drop Soothing Blend in 4 Tbsp. of carrier oil.

Apply 1 drop diluted Soothing Blend to reduce pain daily or as needed.

Diffuse Protective Blend for at least 20-30 minutes 2-3 times daily.

Feed your pet a high quality diet and continue supplementing with Omega-3 and probiotics.

Note: Pyometra is preventable by spaying your dog or cat at a young age, ideally prior to any heat (estrus) cycles.

RESPIRATORY CONDITIONS

Respiratory conditions can be the result of several conditions including viruses, bacteria, fungal organisms, parasites, allergies, heart disease and cancer. Dogs and cats are also affected by second-hand smoke. Most commonly, pets cough, sneeze, wheeze, and suffer from runny eyes and noses. Some pets cough so much that they vomit (See Diarrhea and Vomiting).

Since signs of respiratory illness can indicate many different issues, it is best to see your veterinarian for a physical exam, diagnostic testing and a diagnosis.

"If you think dogs can't count, try putting three dog biscuits in your pocket and then give him only two of them."

- Phil Pastoret

To help your pet breathe more easily and open up airway passages, apply Respiratory Blend, Eucalyptus or Frankincense topically. Diffuse Protective Blend, Respiratory Blend, Eucalyptus or Cleansing Blend for several hours each day and night, especially in the area where your pet sleeps. This will help support the immune system, decrease air-born allergens and germs.

Trouble breathing can be very stressful for you and your pet. Apply and diffuse Calming Blend or Lavender to help keep you and your pet calm. Lavender is also anti-viral and a natural antihistamine, which is beneficial if your pet is suffering from a virus or allergies.

FOR DOGS

Apply 1-2 drops of Respiratory Blend or Eucalyptus and Frankincense 2-4 times daily.

Apply 1-2 drops of lavender to ease stress and in viral cases of respiratory illness.

Diffuse Protective Blend, Respiratory Blend, Eucalyptus or Cleansing Blend for several hours each day and throughout the night, especially in the pet's sleeping area.

Continue to support your pet's immune system with a high quality diet and probiotics.

FOR CATS

Apply 1 drop of Respiratory Blend or Eucalyptus and Frankincense 1-2 times daily. Allow most of the oil to absorb in your palms and pet your cat.

Apply 1 drop of lavender to ease stress and for viral cases of respiratory illness.

Diffuse Protective Blend, Respiratory Blend, Eucalyptus or Cleansing Blend for several hours each day and throughout the night, especially in the pet's sleeping area.

Continue to support your pet's immune system with a high quality diet and probiotics.

RINGWORM

Ringworm is a fungal infection, not a worm. Ringworm affects dogs and cats of all ages, but is most common among kittens. It is highly contagious to people. Signs of Ringworm include hair loss, crusty lesions, and scratching. Lesions tend to be found on the ears, face, and front paws. A diagnosis by your veterinarian is recommended. Ringworm is a persistent infection and the treatment is labor intensive and may take several weeks to months to clear.

Essential oils are highly effective against fungal infections and help to heal skin lesions. The combination of Melaleuca, Myrrh and Lavender have been shown to kill fungal organisms and help to restore and repair skin eruptions.

FOR DOGS

Ringworm is highly contagious, wear gloves while treating or bathing your pet.

Combine 1 drop each Melaleuca, Myrrh and Lavender in 2 Tbsp. of carrier oil. Apply mixture daily to affected areas, using caution to avoid the eyes.

Bathe once to twice weekly using natural essential oil Antiseptic Shampoo (See recipe). Use caution to avoid the eyes. Launder any washcloths, rags, or towels used to bathe your pet separately from any other laundry.

FOR CATS

Ringworm is highly contagious, wear gloves while treating or bathing your pet.

Combine 1 drop each Melaleuca, Myrrh and Lavender in 4 Tbsp. of carrier oil. Apply mixture daily to affected areas.

Bathe once to twice weekly using natural essential oil Antiseptic Shampoo (See recipe). Use caution to avoid the eyes. Launder any washcloths, rags, or towels used to bathe your pet separately from any other laundry.

Since many cats are resistant to bathing, oral antifungal medication may be required to reduce or eliminate the need to bathe your cat.

Antiseptic Shampoo

10 oz. Water

2 oz. Aloe Vera

1 Tbsp. of Castile soap

2 drops of Myrrh Essential Oil

2 drops of Lavender Essential Oil

2 drops of Melaleuca Essential Oil

2 drops Cleansing Blend if directed.

Combine in a jar. Shake well. Lather and rinse well.

SCABIES (SARCOPTIC MANGE)

Scabies is a highly contagious mite which lives in the skin of dogs. Dogs with scabies are usually very itchy, and secondary bacterial infections are common. If you notice skin eruptions, hair loss, or severe scratching, see your veterinarian. Scabies is diagnosed with a physical and microscopic exam. Traditional treatment includes injectable ivermectin, bathing and antibiotics. Scabies can easily infect people, so if any family members have skin irritations or seem itchy, contact your physician.

Complement traditional therapy with essential oils. Essential oils can soothe the skin and prevent infection. Apply Lavender, Cleansing Blend, Myrrh and Helichrysum to the affected areas by petting. Apply Healing Salve and/or Sunburn Spray (See recipe) to lesions to heal skin irritation(s) and reduce itching. Bathing your dog using Soothing Skin Shampoo (See recipe) with 3 drops Cleansing Blend added will help keep the skin clean, heal any skin infections and help to remove flaky skin. Feed your pet a high quality diet, and supplement with Omega-3 and probiotics.

FOR DOGS

Scabies is highly contagious, wear gloves while treating or bathing your pet

Apply 1 drop each of Lavender, Cleansing Blend, Myrrh and Helichrysum twice daily to affected areas or by petting.

Apply Healing Salve 1-2 times daily to localized lesions.

Apply Sunburn Spray 2-4 times daily or as needed.

Bathe with Soothing Shampoo with 3 drops added Cleansing Blend 1-2 times weekly (See recipe). Use caution to avoid the eyes. Launder any washcloths, rags, or towels used to bathe your pet separately from any other laundry.

Feed a high quality diet and supplement with Omega-3 and probiotics.

Sunburn/Skin HealingSpray

4 oz. dark glass spray bottle

1 oz. Purified Water

2-4 drops Lavender Essential Oil

1 drop Helichrysum Essential Oil

½ tsp. Pure Organic Aloe Vera

Place all ingredients in the dark glass spray bottle. Shake well. Spray the affected area, taking caution to avoid your pet's eyes. You may spray some of the mixture into your hands and carefully apply to your pet's face, head and muzzle.

Note: Try to purchase the best quality Aloe Vera possible. Aloe Vera products that contain synthetics will dry the skin and will not help the skin to heal from a sunburn or skin condition.

Healing Salve

8 oz. Cold-Pressed Organic Coconut Oil

1 oz. Beeswax

2 drops Vitamin E (optional)

10 drops Lavender Essential Oil

5 drops Myrrh Essential Oil

3 drops Helichrysum Essential Oil

Glass Jars or Tin Containers

Place the coconut oil and beeswax over a double-boiler, and gently warm over low heat until the beeswax melts. Remove from heat and add the essential oils and Vitamin E oil, (if using). Quickly pour the mixture into glass jars or tins, and allow to cool completely. Store salve in a cool location where they will not re-melt and re-solidify. When stored correctly, salve will last for 1-3 years. Yields 8 oz.

Antiseptic Shampoo

10 oz. Water

2 oz. Aloe Vera

1 Tbsp. of Castile soap

2 drops of Myrrh Essential Oil

2 drops of Lavender Essential Oil

2 drops of Melaleuca Essential Oil

2 drops Cleansing Blend if directed.

Combine in a jar. Shake well. Lather and rinse well.

"Animals are such agreeable friends, they ask no questions, they pass no criticisms."

— George Elliot

Helichrysum

SEIZURES AND NEUROLOGIC CONDITIONS

A variety of conditions can lead to seizures and neurologic disease in dogs and cats. Seizures are most commonly inherited or due to metabolic diseases, hypoglycemia, trauma, toxins, viral infections, and tumors. Seizures occur because of uncontrollable abnormal electrical impulses in the brain. Many of us think of seizures as shaking violently and convulsing, yet some seizures are much more subtle. Seizures may appear as small muscle twitches of the eyelids, whiskers or ears, whole body trembling or uncontrolled movements of one leg.

Neurologic conditions can lead to seizures and are often observed as loss of balance, falling, head tilt, dizziness and abnormal eye movements. These may be the result of hereditary disease, congenital malformations of the brain and spinal column, pain, tick-borne illness, severe or chronic ear infections, vestibular disease and tumors.

> *"Petting, scratching, and cuddling a dog could be as soothing to the mind and heart as deep meditation and almost as good for the soul as prayer."*
> *- Dean Koontz*

If your dog or cat is having a seizure, consult your veterinarian. Use caution when applying oils while your pet is having a seizure.

Frankincense and Helichrysum are especially beneficial and calming to the nervous system. Keeping you and your pet relaxed during a seizure is very important. Several essential oils such as Grounding Blend, Roman Chamomile, Calming Blend, Joyful Blend and Lavender may be used to reduce tension in the home.

Frankincense

FOR DOGS & CATS

Contact your veterinarian immediately.

Be careful applying oils while your pet is having a seizure.

Combine 2 drops each of Frankincense and Helichrysum and 2 drops of any combination of the following essential oils: Grounding Blend, Roman Chamomile, Calming Blend, Joyful Blend or Lavender twice daily.

Diffuse Frankincense, Lavender, or Calming Blend for at least 20-30 minutes 2-3 times daily.

Feed a high quality diet and supplement with Omega-3 and probiotics.

SNAKE BITES

Most snakes are not poisonous but there are a few that cause concern. Snake bites are much more common in dogs than in cats. Some common venomous snakes are the rattlesnake, copperhead, water moccasin and coral snake. If bitten by any of these snakes, take your pet to the veterinarian immediately.

A snake bite is an emergency. Antivenin needs to be administered as soon as possible to minimize the extent of the injury and help the dog recover.

Signs of a snake bite include redness, pain and inflammation at the site of the bite, lethargy, weakness, difficulty breathing, salivation, nausea and bruising of the skin and gums. If you suspect a snake bite, seek medical attention immediately.

In the Event Your Pet is Bitten by a Snake
1. Take your pet to the veterinarian immediately.
2. Stop any bleeding and immobilize the limb if possible.
3. Do not apply ice on the bite.
4. Clean the area carefully and cover if time permits.
5. Keep yourself and your pet calm.

Immediately apply Basil and Melaleuca topically. After your pet has seen the veterinarian, apply Frankincense and Helichrysum to speed healing, coupled with any anti-venom treatment your veterinarian has prescribed. Add either Protective Blend or Lemon to drinking water (if there are no cats in the home). Diffuse and/or apply Grounding Blend, Invigorating Blend or Lavender to help keep you and your pet calm.

Rosemary, found in a protective blend

FOR DOGS & CATS

 Seek Veterinary Care Immediately.

Apply 1-2 drops of Basil and Melaleuca topically (as soon as possible after the snake bite). Repeat every 2 hours until your pet has received medical attention.

After your pet has seen the veterinarian, apply 1-2 drops each of Frankincense and Helichrysum twice daily.

Add 1 drop of either Protective Blend or Lemon to drinking water (if there are no cats in the home).

Diffuse and/or apply Grounding Blend, Invigorating Blend or Lavender to help keep you and your pet calm.

SPIDER BITES

Spiders have their place in the world, and we can certainly appreciate them for keeping away pests such as flies and mosquitos, but that doesn't mean you want them setting up camp in your bedroom or hiding out in your closet. There's no need to turn to insecticides or pesticides. Plenty of natural deterrents are available to keep spiders away from your home and your pets.

Spider bites can result in painful, red, swollen lesions or sores, which may lead to infection. Avoid spiders by using Repellant Blend (See Fleas, Ticks, and Mosquitoes) on your pet daily or as needed. In the event of a spider bite, directly apply Lavender, Melaleuca, Repellant Blend, or Cleansing Blend.

FOR DOGS

Apply 1-2 drops of Lavender, Melaleuca, Repellant Blend, or Cleansing Blend 2-4 times daily or as needed.

FOR CATS

Apply 1-2 drops of Lavender, Repellant Blend, or Cleansing Blend 2-4 times daily or as needed. Alternatively, dilute 1 drop Melaleuca in 4 Tbsp. of carrier oil and apply 1-2 drops 2-4 times daily or as needed.

Spider Control

Diffuse Repellant Blend, Cleansing Blend, Peppermint or Lavender in areas of the home likely to attract spiders such as enclosed porches, basements and attics.

Spray areas in your home with Natural Spider-Stay-Away-Spray. Before using the spray, vacuum any egg sacs or old spider webs using the hose attachment.

Natural Spider-Stay-Away-Spray

5 to 7 drops Peppermint Essential Oil

5-7 drops Melaleuca Essential Oil

5-7 drops Lavender Essential Oil

1 Tbsp. liquid dish soap

1 Tbsp. white vinegar (optional)

16 oz. warm water

glass spray bottle

Put 5-7 drops of each essential oil in a 16 oz. glass spray bottle and fill mostly to the top with warm water. Add 1 tablespoon of natural dish soap, replace the top, and shake the mixture well. Spray the corners of window frames, along door cracks, or in dark, dingy places spiders may be hiding out. You may also add a teaspoon of white vinegar to the mixture, but keep in mind that vinegar may affect some fabrics and surfaces.

THE YOUNG AND THE AGED

In many ways a young pet is very similar to an older pet and requires more care. Young or old pets can benefit from powerful, therapeutic, gentle essential oils.

Frankincense is considered the "life force" essential oil. It is very safe for all ages from newborn to elderly. In this book, you'll notice that Frankincense is mentioned in numerous sections and for a variety of conditions.

Frankincense is one of the oils that crosses the blood-brain barrier, making it useful for neurologic conditions, emotional balance, depression, and in supporting the immune system. Frankincense increases oxygen delivery to cells, aiding in respiratory conditions and normal blood pressure levels.

Frankincense repairs DNA, assisting in treating cancers and autoimmune disease.

Frankincense is anti-inflammatory and anti-infectious.

When in doubt, use Frankincense!

Apply a few drops of Frankincense to your pet daily. This will help to keep your pet healthy, will help to create a bond between you and your pet and will make your young or old pet feel safe.

"I love cats because I enjoy my home; and little by little, they become its visible soul."

- Jean Cocteau

Caring For Your Pet-Young And Old

- Create a comfortable and safe environment for your pet with easy access to food, water, litter box (for cats), and bedding.

- Plenty of regular attention, exercise and affection is good for morale, both yours and your pet's.

- Keep up with routine preventive care such as vaccinations, parasite prevention, dental care and nutritional management.

- Schedule regular wellness exams.

- Monitor your pet and take note of any changes in health or behavior.

- Adjust your pet's nutrition with development and age.

- Make sure your home is at a comfortable temperature.

- Be aware of specific issues relevant to your pet's age and breed.

FOR DOGS & CATS

Apply 1-2 drops of Frankincense to your pet two times per day.

TICK-BORNE DISEASES

Ticks are present throughout the United States. They can transmit several diseases. Ticks tend to bite dogs more commonly than cats. Ticks spread Lyme, Ehrlichiosis, Rocky Mountain Spotted Fever, Anaplasmosis, Tick Paralysis and Cytauxzoonosis. Most of these diseases may also be transferred to people via a tick bite.

If you find a tick on your pet, you (or your veterinarian) may remove it by tweezing around it, as close to the skin as possible. Do not squeeze the tick's body. In removing the entire tick, you may take away some of your dog's skin, since the tick is firmly attached. In either case whether you remove the tick or not, call your veterinarian.

"Dogs are our link to paradise. They don't know evil or jealousy or discontent."

- Milan Kundera

If your dog has contracted a disease from the tick, the signs may not be noticed for several days or weeks. Some common symptoms your pet may exhibit are lethargy, depression, joint pain, reduced activity, decreased appetite, fever, incoordination or pale gums. Monitor your pet closely for any of these symptoms, which may not be apparent for several days to weeks. At any sign of illness, call your veterinarian for a physical exam and appropriate diagnostic testing.

Tick-borne diseases are generally treated with antibiotics. Use essential oils to complement traditional therapy. Apply Cleansing Blend, Lavender, Myrrh and Melaleuca to the area of the tick bite daily and apply Oregano (diluted) and Helichrysum daily. Add

Protective Blend or Lemon to the drinking water (if there are no cats in the home). These oils will help to support the immune system and help to kill any diseases that may have been carried by the tick. Feed your pet a high quality diet and supplement with Omega-3 and probiotics.

For ongoing protection, bathe your pet with natural Flea and Tick Shampoo and apply natural Flea and Tick Repellant Spray (See Fleas, Ticks and Mosquitoes) daily or as needed.

> *"Animals know that the ultimate point of life is to enjoy it."*
>
> *- Samuel Butler*

FOR DOGS

 Call your Veterinarian.

Remove the tick with tweezers very close to the skin. Do not squeeze the tick's body.

Apply 1-2 drops each of Cleansing Blend, Myrrh, Lavender and Melaleuca to the area of the tick bite 2-4 times daily.

Dilute 1 drop of Oregano in 2-4 Tbsp. of carrier oil. Apply 1 drop diluted Oregano and 1-2 drops Helichrysum twice daily.

Add 1 drop Protective Blend or Lemon to 2 cups drinking water (if there are no cats in the home).

Bathe your pet with natural Flea and Tick Shampoo (See recipe), and apply natural Flea and Tick Repellant Spray (See recipe) (See Fleas, Ticks and Mosquitoes) daily or as needed.

Feed your pet a high quality diet and supplement with Omega-3 and probiotics.

Eucalyptus

Flea & Tick Repellent Shampoo or Spray

Add the following to 8 oz. of all natural shampoo base:
4 drops Clary Sage
2 drops Cleansing Blend
5 drops Repellent Blend
8 drops Peppermint
4 drops Lemon
2 drops Geranium
2 drops Eucalyptus
3 drops Lavender
2 drops Myrrh

For spray, simply substitute 8 oz. of purified water for 8 oz. of shampoo base.

Spray your dog, bedding and yourself!

TRAUMA

In the event your pet suffers a severe injury, fall, bleeding, fire or is hit by a car, contact your veterinarian immediately.

Apply pressure to stop any bleeding and immobilize your pet. If you are alone get to a veterinarian as quickly as possible. If you have help begin using essential oils immediately. Helichrysum and Lemon essential oils will help to stop the bleeding. Lavender reduces pain. Soak a gauze pad or soft cloth in 1 cup of warm water containing 1 drop each of Helichrysum, Lemon and Lavender and apply to the wound. After your pet visits the veterinarian, and if your pet has suffered a wound continue using essential oils (See Cuts and Scrapes). Apply Lavender, Helichrysum, Myrrh and Soothing Blend (diluted in cats) daily. Add Helichrysum to drinking water (if there are no cats in the home).

After your dog or cat has been seen by the veterinarian, facilitate healing and reduce pain by diffusing the following oils Helichrysum, Frankincense, Cedarwood, and Lavender. You may choose to use a tent or confine your pet to one room while diffusing for 20 minutes, especially in cases of lung trauma.

"When I am feeling low all I
have to do is watch my cats
and my courage returns."

- Charles Bukowski

FOR DOGS

 Seek Veterinary Attention Immediately

Soak a gauze pad or soft cloth in 1 cup of warm water containing 1 drop each of Helichrysum, Lemon and Lavender and apply to the wound.

Add 1 drop Helichrysum to 2 cups drinking water (if there are no cats in the home).

Apply 1-2 drops each Lavender, Helichrysum, and Myrrh 2-4 times daily.

Apply 1-2 drops Soothing Blend 1-2 times daily.

FOR CATS

 Seek Veterinary Attention Immediately

Apply 1-2 drops each Lavender, Helichrysum, and Myrrh 2-4 times daily.

Dilute 1-2 drops Soothing Blend in 4 Tablespoons of carrier oil and apply 1-2 times daily.

Cedarwood

FOR DOGS & CATS

After your dog or cat has been seen by the veterinarian, facilitate healing and reduce pain by diffusing the following oils using a water diffuser: 3 drops of Helichrysum, 2 drops of Frankincense, 1 drop of Cedarwood, and 1 drop of Lavender. You may choose to use a tent or confine your pet to one room while diffusing for 20 minutes, especially in cases of lung trauma.

For a nebulizer diffuser, combine 15 drops of Helichrysum, 10 drops of Frankincense, 5 drops of Cedarwood, and 5 drops of Lavender in an empty bottle and diffuse for 20 minutes every few hours.

URINARY BLOCKAGE (PRIMARILY MALE CATS)

The inability to urinate is an emergency. If your cat has not urinated in 12-24 hours, contact your veterinarian. This condition is serious and can have detrimental effects on your cat's kidneys and may even result in death. To complement veterinary care, apply diluted Juniper Berry daily.

" Cats are furry waterfalls of grace"

- Layla Morgan Wilde

FOR CATS

  Take your cat to the veterinarian immediately.

Add Juniper Berry in the palm of your hand, allow most of the oil to absorb, and pet your cat daily or add Juniper Berry to the litter box as described in Litter Box Power.

Dilute 1 drop of Soothing Blend in 4 Tbsp. of carrier oil, and apply 1-2 times daily.

Apply 1-2 drops Lavender 1-2 times daily.

Diffuse Protective Blend and Citrus Oils for 20-30 minutes 2-3 times daily.

URINARY CONDITIONS

Both dogs and cats commonly develop bladder infections. The signs are increased frequency of urination, straining to urinate, urinary accidents in the home or, for cats, urinating out of the litter box. Sometimes, the urine is visibly discolored or bloody.

Since the same symptoms may indicate bladder stones or crystals, it is best to see your veterinarian for an examination and appropriate diagnostic testing and treatment. Bladder stones generally require surgical removal. Dietary modification may be necessary based on the type of bladder stone and/or crystals.

Essential oils complement traditional therapy and support a strong immune system. Assist your pet's urinary system with Juniper Berry, Citrus, and Protective Blend essential oils. For dogs, apply Juniper Berry to reduce inflammation and act as a diuretic and Soothing blend daily to reduce pain. Add Lemon or Grapefruit to the drinking water (if there are no cats in the home) and diffuse Protective Blend or Citrus oils to rid toxins and support the immune system. Administer a probiotic and omega-3 supplement for overall health.

For cats, place Juniper Berry in the palm of your hand, allow most of the oil to absorb, and pet your cat daily. Juniper Berry may also be added to the litter box as described in Litter Box Power. For pain, apply a mixture of lavender and Soothing Blend diluted in carrier oil daily.

Juniper Berry

FOR DOGS

Apply 1-2 drops Juniper Berry twice daily.

Apply 1-2 drops of Soothing Blend 1-2 times daily.

Add 1 drop Lemon or Grapefruit to two cups drinking water (if there are no cats in the home).

Diffuse Protective Blend or Citrus oils for 20-30 minutes 2-3 times daily.

FOR CATS

Add Juniper Berry in the palm of your hand, allow most of the oil to absorb, and pet your cat daily or add Juniper Berry to the litter box as described in Litter Box Power.

Dilute 1 drop of Soothing Blend in 4 Tbsp. of carrier oil, and apply 1-2 times daily.

Apply 1-2 drops Lavender 1-2 times daily.

Diffuse Protective Blend or citrus oils for 20-30 minutes 2-3 times daily.

URINATING OUTSIDE OF THE LITTER BOX

Cats may refuse to use the litter box for a number of reasons. Some possible causes include painful urination such as a urinary tract infection (See Urinary Conditions). In other cases, your cat may be expressing his or her disapproval of the type of box, or litter, location or cleanliness of the box. He or she may also be expressing feelings of stress, anger or fear (See Anxiety). Many cats prefer having the choice of one of several boxes in different locations. On some occasions, a cat may associate a negative event or noise with the litter box and subsequently, avoid it. A rule of thumb is to provide one litter box per cat plus one extra. Scoop the boxes at least once daily. Fully clean the boxes and change the litter weekly.

If indicated, visit your veterinarian for a thorough physical exam and appropriate diagnostic testing and medical treatment.

Apply lavender to your cat daily for stress and anxiety. Diffuse Grounding Blend, Calming Blend, or Lavender for calming or Cleansing Blend for odor elimination. Add Grounding Blend, Calming Blend, Lavender or Cleansing Blend to the litter box as described in Litter Box Power. Clean your home with Protective Blend natural cleaners.

FOR CATS

Apply 1-2 drops Lavender once daily.

Diffuse Grounding Blend, Cleansing Blend, Calming Blend or Lavender for 20-30 minutes 2-3 times daily.

Add Grounding Blend, Cleansing Blend, Calming Blend or Lavender to the litter box (See Litter Box Power).

Clean with Protective Blend Cleaner Concentrate.

Litter Box Power

Add 1-2 drops of the chosen essential oil (ex. Digestive Blend, Lavender, Cleansing Blend, Lemongrass, or Orange) to 1 cup of baking soda.

Allow the mixture to rest overnight in a glass jar.

Add 1 tablespoon of the mixture of essential oil and baking soda recipe to the litter box daily.

VAGINITIS

Vaginitis is an infection or inflammation of the vagina and is most common in developing puppies. Vaginitis may result from bacterial, viral or fungal infections. Obesity also contributes to increased risk of vaginitis.

Signs of vaginitis include excessive licking of the genital area, increased frequency of urinations, difficulty housebreaking and vaginal discharge. Clean your dog's vaginal area daily with Gentle Cleanser (See recipe). Apply Melaleuca and Lavender daily. Diffuse Protective Blend. Add Lemon to drinking water, (if there are no cats in the home). Feed your pet a high quality diet and supplement with Omega-3 and probiotics.

If signs of vaginitis persist for more than 2-3 days, contact your veterinarian.

FOR DOGS

Clean your dog's vaginal area 2-4 times daily with Gentle Cleanser (See recipe).

Apply 1 drop each Melaleuca and Lavender twice daily.

Diffuse Protective Blend for at least 20-30 minutes 2-3 times daily.

Add 1 drop Lemon to 2 cups drinking water, (if there are no cats in the home).

Feed your pet a high quality diet and supplement with Omega-3 and probiotics.

If signs of vaginitis persist for more than 2-3 days, contact your veterinarian.

Gentle Cleanser

4 oz. Castile soap or unscented natural foaming soap
2 drops Roman Chamomile Essential Oil
2 drops Lavender Essential Oil

WORMS/INTESTINAL PARASITES

Nearly all puppies and kittens are born with intestinal parasites, which they get from their mother. The parasites appear during pregnancy and nursing. Young puppies and kittens are normally dewormed by their veterinarian, yet they may become infected with intestinal parasites at any time throughout their lives. Worms may be transmitted by the feces of other dogs and cats or found in contaminated areas. Worms may even enter our homes on our shoes. Intestinal tapeworms are also transmitted by fleas (See Fleas, Ticks, and Mosquitoes). You may notice worms in the feces when you clean up after your pets. Pets may also develop diarrhea. See your veterinarian for physical and diagnostic testing.

"There's no need for a piece of sculpture in a home that has a cat."

-Wesley Bates

Be particularly cautious in areas where dogs may congregate or play together, such as parks. Responsible pet owners should clean up after their dogs and properly dispose of waste. Stray cats may deposit worms wherever they roam.

Many types of intestinal worms are also contagious to people. Children are at a higher risk than adults, since they are not as conscientious about cleanliness. Protect yourself and your family by practicing good hygiene. Wash your hands after cleaning up messes, cleaning the litter box or picking up after your pet. Wash your hands prior to cooking, preparing food or eating. Keep children away from the litter box and other dirty areas (See Natural Hand Sanitizer recipe).

Essential oils will complement traditional therapies and support the immune system.

For dogs, apply Digestive Blend and Melaleuca daily. Add Protective Blend or Lemon to drinking water (if there are no cats in the home). Diffuse Protective Blend or Lemon, alternating oils if you wish.

For cats, apply Melaleuca (diluted), Lavender and Myrrh daily. Diffuse Protective Blend or Lemon, alternating oils if you wish.

FOR DOGS

Apply 1 drop Digestive Blend 1-2 times daily.

Apply 1 drop Melaleuca 1-2 times daily.

Add 1 drop of Protective Blend or Lemon to 2 cups drinking water (if there are no cats in the home).

Diffuse Protective Blend and Lemon for 20-30 minutes 2-3 times daily, alternating oils.

FOR CATS

Dilute 1 drop Melaleuca in 4 Tbsp. carrier oil and apply 1 drop daily.

Apply 1 drop each Lavender and Myrrh 1-2 times daily.

Diffuse Protective Blend and Lemon for 20-30 minutes 2-3 times daily, alternating oils.

COMMONLY RECOMMENDED ESSENTIAL OILS FOR PETS

Bergamot, historically was used for fevers and digestive tract problems. It is antibacterial and an antiseptic and has been shown to be effective in treating urinary tract infections. Bergamot is excellent for skin care, and like many citrus oils, is calming and helpful for anxiety and depression. It is uplifting and energizing. (found in Invigorating Blend)

Cedarwood is useful for respiratory conditions, skin issues, as well as kidney and urinary tract problems. Cedarwood is high in a natural chemical called cedrol. Cedrol has been found to enhance fibroblast growth in the skin and it is very good for skin recovery. Cedarwood promotes restfulness, feelings of calmness and relaxation.

Citrus oils are uplifting, energizing, useful for stimulating appetite, supporting the immune system and relieving anxiety. Lemon increases the effectiveness of white blood cells, a type of immune cells. (found in Cleansing Blend and Respiratory Blend) Grapefruit is high in a compound called d-limonene, which is beneficial in cancer prevention and support.

Chamomile (Roman) is an essential oil that has been used for centuries for a broad range of applications including, allergies, burns, diarrhea, nausea, psoriasis, sprains, fever, earaches, teething, and stomach aches. It is beneficial for many skin conditions, including burns, cuts, abrasions and insect bites. Roman Chamomile has calming and relaxing properties. It can help with anxiety, depression, insomnia, and restlessness. (found in Calming Blend)

Cypress is particularly beneficial for improving circulation and for lymphatic drainage. Cypress may also be useful for strengthening blood capillary walls, the circulatory system, edema, lung circulation, liver disorders, and wounds. (found in Massage Blend).

Eucalyptus is known for respiratory support and is useful for allergies, asthma, colds, and fevers. It not only helps relieve the symptoms but also has antibacterial and antiviral properties. It is also helpful to repel pests. (found in Respiratory Blend, and Repellant Blend)

Frankincense is a wondrous oil. It is beneficial for numerous conditions and body systems. Use Frankincense for neurologic disorders, autoimmune disorders, respiratory illness, depression, and to restore life force. Frankincense has been extensively studied for it's anti-tumoral properties. When in doubt, use Frankincense. (found in Grounding Blend and Anti-aging Blend)

Geranium is used heavily in the perfume and cosmetic industry. For this reason, it is important to be assured of the purity and quality of the essential oil that you are using, since there are lower quality products easily available. Pure therapeutic grade Geranium aids hormonal balance, reduces inflammation and bruises, is antiseptic and aids in treatment of ear infections and is beneficial for the skin. (found in Detoxification Blend)

Helichrysum contains natural chemicals that renew and calm tissue. It has anti-fungal and antimicrobial properties and is helpful for respiratory illnesses, skin conditions, painfulness and neurologic conditions. Specifically, it is useful for skin irritations, bruising, sprains and joint or arthritic pain. It has very strong anti-inflammatory properties and has been known to aid in blood circulation and hypertension. Helichrysum is also beneficial in the detoxification and stimulation of liver cell function. (found in Soothing Blend, Anti-aging Blend)

Lavender is a versatile oil known for its calming properties. Lavender is an adaptogen, meaning it can assist the body when adapting to stress or imbalances. It is a natural antihistamine, antiviral, and helpful for dry skin, burns, bruises, cuts, and wounds. (found in Calming Blend and Anti-aging Blend)

Lemongrass is beneficial for thyroid conditions and for hormonal balance. It is a very effective pain reliever, kills fungal infections, and deters pests. (found in Repellant Blend)

Melaleuca (hot oil) is a powerful antiseptic oil. Use melaleuca to help fight viruses, bacteria and fungal infections. Melaleuca, also known as Tea Tree oil, is well known for it's cleansing and soothing properties and is beneficial for treating wounds and skin conditions. (found in Cleansing Blend and Respiratory Blend)

Myrrh stimulates the immune system and blood circulation. Thus, Myrrh helps to relieve pain, subdue swelling and promote tissue regeneration and is a potent antimicrobial, analgesic, useful in thyroid conditions, cancer, diabetes, digestive issues and wounds. (found in Anti-aging Blend)

Oregano (hot oil) is a powerful anti-inflammatory. It is nature's antibiotic, effective against MRSA and other infectious agents. Oregano is also powerful against viruses, fungal organisms, bacteria, parasites and warts.

Peppermint is soothing for painful conditions, indigestion, vomiting, diarrhea, congestion, fever, and allergies. It is beneficial in dental care due to its antiseptic properties and ability to clear the respiratory tract and ease breathing. It has also been found to improve concentration and mental sharpness. (found in Respiratory Blend, Digestive Blend and Soothing Blend)

Sandalwood promotes a feeling of calm and is useful in depression, anxiety, cancer and dry skin conditions. (found in Anti-aging Blend)

Wintergreen is helpful in reducing pain and inflammation. It can be used for respiratory conditions, arthritis, and headaches. (found in Soothing Blend)

Ylang Ylang is useful as an antidepressant and promotes feelings of calmness. It helps to alleviate feelings of anger and fear. Ylang Ylang also helps to regulate blood pressure and hormones. Historically, it was used for skin treatments, insect bites, hair loss, digestive issues and for the respiratory system. (found in Joyful Blend)

Note: Cassia and Black Pepper are hot oils and are only recommended in this book for deterring pets from chewing and destructive behavior. These oils have many uses but we do not recommend their use in pets.

Ylang Ylang

RECIPES

Antiseptic Shampoo

10 oz. Water

2 oz. Aloe Vera

1 Tbsp. of Castile soap

2 drops of Myrrh Essential Oil

2 drops of Lavender Essential Oil

2 drops of Melaleuca Essential Oil

2 drops Cleansing Blend if directed.

Combine in a jar. Shake well. Lather and rinse well.

Chew Deterrent Spray with Essential Oils

Add 5-6 drops of Cassia, Black Pepper, or citrus essential oil to a 4 oz. glass spray bottle and fill with water. Shake the bottle well to mix. Test the spray on a hidden area of your furniture (or other object which your puppy/dog likes to chew) to ensure it will not stain or mark the item. Spray generously and reapply as the smell wears off. If the spray does not seem to be working well, add more of the essential oil or prepare the Chew Deterrent Spray with a different hot essential oil.

Flea & Tick Repellent Shampoo or Spray

Add the following to 8 oz. of all natural shampoo base:

4 drops Clary Sage Essential Oil

2 drops Cleansing Essential Oil Blend

5 drops Outdoor Essential Oil Blend

8 drops Peppermint Essential Oil

4 drops Lemon Essential Oil

2 drops Geranium Essential Oil

2 drops Eucalyptus Essential Oil

3 drops Lavender Essential Oil

2 drops Myrrh Essential Oil

For spray, simply substitute 8 oz. of purified water for 8 oz. of shampoo base.

Spray your dog, bedding and yourself!

Gentle Cleanser
4 ounces Castile soap or unscented natural foaming soap
2 drops Roman Chamomile Essential Oil
2 drops Lavender Essential Oil

Healing Salve
8 ounces Cold-Pressed Organic Coconut Oil
1 ounce Beeswax
2 drops Vitamin E (optional)
10 drops Lavender Essential Oil
5 drops Myrrh Essential Oil
3 drops Helichrysum Essential Oil
Glass Jars or Tin Containers
Place the coconut oil and beeswax over a double –boiler, and gently warm over low heat until the beeswax melts. Remove from heat and add the essential oils and Vitamin E oil, (if using). Quickly pour the mixture into glass jars or tins, and allow to cool completely. Store salve in a cool location where it will not re-melt and re-solidify. When stored correctly, salve will last for 1-3 years. Yields 8 oz.

Healing Spray and Healing Oil Blend

4 oz. glass spray bottle

15 drops Frankincense Essential Oil

10 drops Oregano Essential Oil (substitute Geranium Essential Oil for cats)

10 drops Lavender Essential Oil

10 drops Helichrysum Essential Oil

4 oz. of water for the spray OR

100 drops of carrier oil such as Fractionated Coconut Oil

Homemade Flea Collar

Mix 4 oz. of distilled water with 10 drops Eucalyptus, 10 drops Repellent Blend and 10 drops Lemongrass Essential Oils.

Soak a nylon collar in the solution for 20 minutes.

Remove collar and allow it to dry thoroughly before placing it on your pet.

Re-soak the collar every two weeks or more frequently as needed.

Litter Box Power

Add 1-2 drops of the chosen essential oil (ex. Digestive Blend, Lavender, Cleansing Blend, Lemongrass, or Wild Orange) to 1 cup of baking soda.

Allow the mixture to rest overnight in a glass jar.

Add 1 Tbsp. of the mixture of essential oil and baking soda recipe to the litter box daily.

Natural Ear Cleaner

1 oz. Witch Hazel

1 oz. Apple Cider Vinegar

Sometimes referred to as nature's antibiotic ointment, witch hazel can be effective in cleaning your pet's ears while protecting them from further infection. This natural remedy, produced from the leaves and bark of the North American witch hazel shrub, encourages quicker healing of minor breaks in skin and has proven anti-inflammatory properties.

Used for decades in folk medicine, apple cider vinegar has been proven to kill germs and heal naturally.

Natural Flea Bomb

10 drops Black Pepper Essential Oil

10 drops Oregano Essential Oil

10 drops Wild Orange Essential Oil

10 drops Peppermint Essential Oil

10 drops Cleansing Essential Oil Blend (to be used after "flea bombing" the house)

Add 10 drops each of Black Pepper, Oregano, Wild Orange and Peppermint Essential Oils to a water diffuser or in an empty bottle for a nebulizer diffuser. Open all of the interior doors in your home and place the diffuser in the most central location possible. If there is a heavy infestation in more than one room, you will need to treat each room individually. Turn your diffuser on to maximum output and use a continuous diffusion for 2-3 hours. Leave your home during this time. Upon returning home, open all of the windows in your home. Diffuse Cleansing Blend for another 1-2 hours. Now, it is time to vacuum everywhere! Move furniture to vacuum behind it and under it. Vacuum the furniture, too. Empty the vacuum when you are finished.

Natural Hand Sanitizer

5 Tbsp. Aloe Vera Gel

4 Tbsp. water

1/4 tsp. Vitamin E oil

8-10 drops of Protective Essential Oil Blend

Wisk together all of the ingredients and place in a spray or squeeze bottle for use on the go.

Note: Essential oils can be stored in plastic containers if the essential oils are of high quality and highly diluted.

Natural Spider-Stay-Away-Spray

5 to 7 drops Peppermint Essential Oil

5-7 drops Melaleuca Essential Oil

5-7 drops Lavender Essential Oil

1 Tbsp. liquid dish soap

1 Tbsp. white vinegar (optional)

16 oz. warm water

glass spray bottle

Put 5-7 drops of each essential oil in a 16 oz. glass spray bottle and fill mostly to the top with warm water. Add 1 tablespoon of natural dish soap, replace the top, and shake the mixture well. Spray the corners of window frames, along door cracks, or in dark, dingy places spiders may be hiding out. You may also add a teaspoon of white vinegar to the mixture, but keep in mind that vinegar may affect some fabrics and surfaces.

Pet Powder

1 Cup Corn Starch

5 drops Lavender Essential Oil

5 drops Geranium Essential Oil

4 drops Eucalyptus Essential Oil

Mix well, and keep in a small mason jar with several holes in the top. Sprinkle a small amount on your dog and brush him or her. He or she will not only smell great, but repels ticks and other pests.

Soothing Skin Shampoo

3 oz. Castile soap (available at many health and bulk food stores)

2 oz. Organic unpasteurized, unfiltered Apple Cider Vinegar

1 oz. Vegetable Glycerin

2 oz. Distilled water

3 drops Lavender Essential Oil

3 drops Chamomile Essential Oil

Optional: add 1 tsp. ground oatmeal

Sunburn/Skin Healing Spray

4 oz. dark glass spray bottle

1 oz. Purified Water

2-4 drops Lavender Essential Oil

1 drop Helichrysum Essential Oil

½ tsp. Pure Organic Aloe Vera

Place all ingredients in the dark glass spray bottle. Shake well. Spray the affected area, taking caution to avoid your pet's eyes. You may spray some of the mixture into your hands and carefully apply to your pet's face, head and muzzle.

Note: Try to purchase the best quality Aloe Vera possible. Aloe Vera products that contain synthetics will dry the skin and will not help the skin to heal from a sunburn or skin condition.

REFERENCES

Bae GS, Park KC, Choi SB, Et Al. Protective effects of alpha-pinene in mice with cerulein-induced acute pancreatitis. Life Sci. 2012;91(17-18):866-871.

Bell KL, (2002) Holistic Aromatherapy for Animals: A Comprehensive Guide to the Use of Essential Oils & Hydrosols with Animals, Forres Scotland, UK Findhorn Press

Chen Y, Zhou C, Ge Z, et al. Composition and potential anticancer activities of essential oils obtained from myrrh and frankincense. Oncol Lett. 2013;6(4):1140-1146.

Chin KB, Cordell B. The effect of tea tree oil (Melaleuca alternifolia) on wound healing using a dressing model. J Altern Complement Med. 2013;19(12):942-945.

Crowell P. L. and Gould M. N., Chemoprevention and therapy of cancer by d-limonene. Crit Rev. Oncog. 5 (1):1-22, 1994.

de Sousa AA, Soares PM, de Almeida AN, et al. Antispasmodic effect of Mentha piperita essential oil on tracheal smooth muscle of rats. J Ethnopharmacol. 2010;130(2):422-436.

Elegbede J.A., Elson C. E., Qureshi A., Tanner M. A., and Gould M. N., Inhibition of DMBA induced mammary cancer by the monoterpene d-limonene. Carcinogenesis 5 (5):661-664, 1984

Elson C. E., Maltzman T. H., Boston J. L., Tanner M. A., and Gould M. N., Anti-carcinogenic activity of d-limonene during the initiation and promotion/progression stages of DMBA-induced rat mammary carcinogenesis. Carcinogenesis 9 (2):331-332, 1988.

Fan AY, Lao L, Zhang RX, Et Al. Effects of an acetone extract of Boswellia carterii Birdw. (Burseraceae) gum resin on adjuvant-induced arthritis in lewis rats. J Ethnopharmacol. 2005;101(1-3):104-109.

Frank MB1, Yang Q, Osban J, Azzarello JT, Saban MR, Saban R, Ashley RA, Welter JC, Fung KM, Lin HK. Frankincense oil derived from Boswellia carteri induces tumor cell specific cytotoxicity. BMC Complement Altern Med. 2009 Mar 18;9:6

Gilani AH1, Jabeen Q, Khan AU, Shah AJ. Gut modulatory, blood pressure lowering, diuretic and sedative activities of cardamom. J Ethnopharmacol. 2008 Feb 12;115(3):463-72. Graham L, Wells, DL, Hepper PG. The influence of olfactory stimulation on the behaviour of dogs housed in a rescue shelter. Appl Anim Behav Sci. 2005;91(1-2):143-153.

Haag J. D., Lindstrom M. J., and Gould M. N., Limonene-induced regression of mammary carcinomas. Cancer Res. 52 (14):4021-4026, 1992.

Hancianu M, Cioanca O, Mihasan M, et al. Neuroprotective effects of inhaled lavender oil on scopolamine-induced dementia via anti-oxidative activities in rats. Phytomedicine. 2013;20(5):446-452.

Holmes C, Hopkins V, Hensford C, et al. Lavender oil as a treatment for agitated behaviour in severe dementia: a placebo controlled study. International Journal of Geriatric Psychiatry . 2002;17:305-308.

Homburger, F., Treger, A., Boger, E., Inhibition of Murine Subcutaneous and Intravenous Benzo(rst) Pentaphene. Carcinogenesis by Sweet Orange Oils and D-Limonene. Oncology, 25(1):1-10, 1971.

Hsu WS, Yen JH, Wang YS. Formulas of components of citronella oil against mosquitoes (Aedes aegypti). J Environ Sci Health B. 2013;48(11): 1014-1019.

Jimbo D, Kimura Y, Taniguchi M, et al. Effect of aromatherapy on patients with Alzheimer's disease. Phychogeriatrics. 2009;9(4):173-179.

Johannessen B. Nurses experience of aromatherapy use with dementia patients experiencing disturbed sleep patterns. An action research project. Complement Ther Clin Pract. 2013;19(4):209-213.

Kannappan S, Jayaraman T, Rajasekar P, et al. Cinnamon bark extract improves glucose metabolism and lipid profile in the fructose-fed rat. Singapore Med J. 2006;47(10):858-863.

Kim HM, Cho SH. Lavender oil inhibits immediate-type allergic reaction in mice and rats. J Pharm Pharmacol. 1999; 51(2):221-226.

Koca Kutlu A, Ceçen D, Gürgen SG, Et Al. A Comparison Study of Growth Factor Expression following Treatment with Transcutaneous Electrical Nerve Stimulation, Saline Solution, Povidone-Iodine, and Lavender Oil in Wounds Healing. Evid Based Complement Alternat Med. 2013;2013:361832.

Lai TK, Cheung MC, Lo CK, et al. Effectiveness of aroma massage on advanced cancer patients with constipation: a pilot study. Complement Ther Clin Pract. 2011;17(1):37-43.

Lawal HO, Adewuyi GO, Fawehinmi AB. Chemical evaluation of mosquito repellent formulation prepared from the essential oil of plants. J Nat Products. 2013;6:33-37.

Lin PW, Chan WC, Ng BF, et al. Efficacy of aromatherapy (Lavandula angustifolia) as an intervention for agitated behaviours in Chinese older persons with dementia: a cross-over randomized trial. International Journal of Geriatric Psychiatry. 2007 Mar 7.

Lv YX, Zhao SP, Zhang JY, et al. Effect of orange peel essential oil on oxidative stress in AOM animals. Int J Biol Macromol. 2012;50(4): 1144-1150.

Martinez K, De Santiago L, Care S, et al. Antibacterial Effects of commercial essential oils on bacteria. J Nat Sci. 2012;1(1):1-3.

Martinez-Velazquez M, Castillo-Herrera GA, Rosario-Cruz R. Acaricidal effect and chemical composition of essential oils extracted from Cuminum cyminum, Pimenta dioica and Ocimum basilicum against the cattle tick Rhipicephalus (Boophilus) microplus (Acari: Ixodidae). Parasitol Res. 2011;108(2):481-487.

McKay DL, Blumberg JB. A review of the bioactivity and potential health benefits of peppermint tea (Mentha piperita L.). Phytother Res. 2006;20(8):619-633.

Mishra A, Bhatti R, Singh A, Et Al. Ameliorative effect of the cinnamon oil from Cinnamomum zeylanicum upon early stage diabetic nephropathy. Planta Med. 2010;76(5):412-417.

Misner BD. A novel aromatic oil compound inhibits microbial overgrowth on feet: a case study. J Int Soc Sports Nutr. 2007;4:3.

Modern Essentials: The Contemporary Guide to Therapeutic Use of Essential Oils (5th Ed 2013) Orem, UT, AromaTools

Moon SE, Kim HY, Cha JD. Synergistic effect between clove oil and its major compounds and antibiotics against oral bacteria. Arch Oral Biol. 2011;56(9):907-916.

Moore, C.J.. Kerman, W.S., Wang, B.C., Gould, M.N., Inhibition of Ras-induced mammary carcinogenesis by limonene. Proc Am Assoc Cancer Res, 32:131, 1991.

Moussaieff A, Shein NA, Tsenter J. Incensole acetate: a novel neuroprotective agent isolated from Boswellia carterii. J Cereb Blood Flow Metab. 2008;28(7):1341-1352.

Mugnaini L, Nardoni S, Pinto L, Pistelli L, Leonardi M, Pisseri F, Mancianti F. In vitro and in vivo antifungal activity of some essential oils against feline isolates of Microsporum canis. J Mycol Med. 2012 Jun;22(2):179-84.

Ni X, Suhail MM, Yang Q, Cao A, Fung KM, Postier RG, Woolley C, Young G, Zhang J, Lin HK. Frankincense essential oil prepared from hydrodistillation of Boswellia sacra gum resins induces human pancreatic cancer cell death in cultures and in a xenograft murine model. BMC Complement Altern Med. 2012 D;12:253.

Nomicos EY. Myrrh: medical marvel or myth of the Magi? Holist Nurs Pract. 2007;21(6):308-323.

Nostro A, Blanco AR, Cannatelli MA, Et Al. Susceptibility of methicillinresistant staphylococci to oregano essential oil, carvacrol and thymol. FEMS Microbiol Lett. Jan;230(2):191-195.

O'Flaherty LA, van Dijk M, Albertyn R, Et Al. Aromatherapy massage seems to enhance relaxation in children with burns: an observational pilot study. Burns. 2012;38(6):840-845.

Pepeljnjak S, Kosalec I, Kalodera Z, et al. Antimicrobial activity of juniper berry essential oil (Juniperus communis L., Cupressaceae). Acta Pharm. 2005;55(4):417-422.

Picon PD, Picon RV, Costa AF, et al. Randomized clinical trial of a phytotherapic compound containing Pimpinella anisum, Foeniculum vulgare, Sambucus nigra, and Cassia augustifolia for chronic constipation. BMC Complement Altern Med. 2010;10:17(1-9).

Ritter AM, Domiciano TP, Verri WA Jr, Et Al. Antihypernociceptive activity of anethole in experimental inflammatory pain. Inflammopharmacology. 2013;21(2):187-197.

Sala A, Recio M, Giner RM, et al. Anti-inflammatory and antioxidant properties of Helichrysum italicum. J Pharm Pharmacol. 2002;54(3): 365-371.

Setzer WN. Essential oils and anxiolytic aromatherapy. Nat Prod Commun. 2009;4(9):1305-1316.

Shelton M, (2012) The Animal Desk Reference: Essential Oils for Animals, Howard Lake, MN

Shen J, Niijima A, Tanida M, et al. Olfactory stimulation with scent of lavender oil affects autonomic nerves, lipolysis and appetite in rats. Neurosci Lett. 2005;383(1-2):188-193.

Singh D, Kumar TR, Gupt VK, Et Al. Antimicrobial activity of some promising plant oils, molecules and formulations. Indian J Exp Biol. 2012;50(10):714-717.

Srivastava JK, Shankar E, Gupta S. Chamomile: A herbal medicine of the past with bright future. Mol Med Rep. 2010;3(6):895-901.

Talpur N, Echard B, Ingram C et al. Effects of a novel formulation of essential oils on glucose-insulin metabolism in diabetic and hypertensive rats: a pilot study. Diabetes Obes Metab. 2005; 7(2):193-199.

Thorsell W, Mikiver A, Tunón H. Repelling properties of some plant materials on the tick Ixodes ricinus L.. Phytomedicine. 2006;13(1-2): 132-134.

Ueno-Iio T, Shibakura M, Yokota K et al. Lavender essential oil inhalation suppresses allergic airway inflammation and mucous cell hyperplasia in a murine model of asthma. Life Sci. 2014

Volhard W, Brown, K, (2000) Holistic Guide for a Healthy Dog (2nd Ed), Hobokre, NJ, Wiley Publishing House

Wallenberg, L.W., Coccia, J.B., Inhibition of 4-(methylnitrosamino)-1-(3-pyridyl)-1-butanone Carcinogenesis in Mice by D-Limonene and Citrus Fruit Oils. Carcinogenesis, Vol. 12, No. 1, pp.115-117, 1991

Wells DL. Aromatherapy for travel-induced excitement in dogs. J Am Vet Med Assoc. 2006;229(6):964-967.

Woollard AC, Tatham KC, Barker S. The influence of essential oils on the process of wound healing: a review of the current evidence. J Wound Care. 2007;16(6):255-257.

Yavari Kia P, Safajou F, Shahnazi M, Et Al. The effect of lemon inhalation aromatherapy on nausea and vomiting of pregnancy: a double-blinded, randomized, controlled clinical trial. Iran Red Crescent Med J. 2014;16(3):e14360.